coastal retreats

LINDA LEIGH PAUL

coastal retreats

the pacific northwest *and the* architecture of adventure

UNIVERSE

First published in the United States of America in 2002
by UNIVERSE PUBLISHING
A Division of Rizzoli International Publications, Inc.
300 Park Avenue South
New York, NY 10010

2002 2003 2004 2005 2006 / 10 9 8 7 6 5 4 3 2 1

Printed in China
DESIGNED BY Sara E. Stemen

LIBRARY OF CONGRESS CATALOGING-IN-PUBLICATION DATA

Paul, Linda Leigh.
 Coastal retreats : the Pacific Northwest and the architecture of
adventure / Linda Leigh Paul.
   p. cm.
 ISBN 0-7893-0801-0 (hardcover : alk. paper)
 1. Vacation homes--Northwest, Pacific. 2. Architecture--
Northwest,
Pacific--20th century. I. Title.
 NA7575 .P379 2003
 728.7'2'09795--dc21
                        2002009539

CONTENTS

ACKNOWLEDGMENTS

I AM GRATEFUL for the generosity and kindness of everyone who helped me to complete this book. Many of them had to overcome the constraints of time, institutions, and the climate of the great Pacific Northwest. Their willingness to outrun the impossible was remarkable; I hope it is its own best reward.

I would like to thank the following people for their help and support: Ben Williams, the "archangel of archives" at the Field Museum Library in Chicago; Nathalie Guénette of the *Archives Photographiques* at the *Musée Canadien des Civilisations*, Quebec; Dan Savard of the Royal British Columbia Museum, Victoria, British Columbia; Carolyn Marr of the Museum of History and Industry in Seattle; Chris Kinsey at the University of Washington Library Special Collections Archives; and the staff of the photo archives department at the Oregon History Center in Portland.

Peter Belluschi, who shared his collection of photographs and historical documents of the Harry Wentz studio, gave his time and hospitality generously and deserves warm thanks for directing us through the ice and snow to the welcome of a warm fire on several February days. John Storrs offered reflections on his career and thoughts on architecture and the Northwest in a home that illustrates them perfectly.

I would like to thank the many homeowners who gladly opened their secret retreats to us, and the many architects who contributed their time and shared their knowledge of how to live in the Pacific Northwest. I owe a particular debt to the architectural photographers whose work appears on these pages, and whose contributions enhance this book.

Chris Lee at BOORA Architects, Karen Thurman at Allied Works Architecture, and Cassandra Montgomery of George Suyama Architects offered valuable insights.

I would like to express my admiration for Alexandra Tart, senior editor at Rizzoli/Universe, for her skill and her poise, and for Rizzoli/Universe's outstanding publisher, Charles Miers.

Robert Paul, critic and partner, is a continuing source of amazement.

INTRODUCTION
coastal retreats

The Pacific Ocean as viewed from the cliff-side balcony of the Wentz/Belluschi Studio on Neahkahnie Mountain.

I try to learn the densities of earth
and settle down with style;
An island in the mouth of the
Columbia arrows the way: west.
The pilot tells us "there is some
weather between us and Seattle,"
terrifying to think of there being
none.

—Lisa M. Steinman, "Calling Upon the Night" [1]

THE PACIFIC NORTHWEST is rarely, if ever, discussed without considering its weather. Any suggestion of "there being none," as poet Lisa Steinman knows, is indeed frightening. Northwesterners are obsessed by the climate. On December 16, 1805, the explorer William Clark entered the following into his journal: *"The winds violent. Trees falling in every direction, whorl winds, with gusts of rain Hail & Thunder, this kind of weather lasted all day. Certainly one of the worst days that ever was!"* [2] Had Lewis and Clark stayed on, there would have been other days to compare that day to; perhaps it wasn't as bad as it seemed. Today, for instance, was a day just like the one Clark described, except that there were two inches of snow, too, and tomorrow is the first day of spring.

The term "vacation architecture" seems almost redundant in a place where day-to-day living is itself an outdoor adventure. Reaching most destinations without getting soaked requires dependable outdoor gear, and seasonal hibernations are as much a part of life as the quick exchanges of gear by which rock climbers, stream fishers, windsurfers, glider pilots, cyclists, snowboarders, beachcombers, and rain walkers *undo* themselves. Everyone, it seems, takes part in this year-round game of transformation.

The retreats featured in this book accommodate the shifting needs of people who travel from seashore to mountains or from islands to desert, and whose recreations change with the season and the altitude. Apparent in all of the houses is an unflappable respect for *place*. Designing shelter for the Northwest is as bold an adventure as any other exploration of its terrain, and herein lies a curiosity. How could one expect a single architectural "tradition" to derive from desert, rainforest, beach, alpine, and valley settings in the north temperate zone? One couldn't, of course. But there are traditions belonging to each setting and to the misty blue outlines in the distance.

Retreat architecture in the Northwest defines the human scale within a tenebrous and monumental landscape that dwarfs even the notion of the Burkean sublime, of which the ruling principle is terror. It is a remedy for the adrenaline rushes of *"the thrill that comes of danger, darkness, and solitude, the noisy vastness of cataracts, the fury of raging storms."* [3]

Retreat architecture is absolution. It shows us that to *settle down in style* means to rearrange our thoughts about the measures of modern, period, or high-tech fashion architecture, and even of vernacular and indigenous codes of conduct. The Northwest is an immense realm containing much of this country's most raw and rarely seen land: ragged mountains, hot desert updrafts, spires of volcanic rock dating back seventeen million years, seventy-miles-per-hour winds, misty beaches, painted cliffs, shaded forests.

Unlike the First Nation peoples—the Haida, Chinook, and Nootka—who conjured words for the quick phenomena of nature, most of today's inhabitants of the Northwest no longer have words to describe the green-gold-silver cellophane of sunlight that bounces back into the sky from the steaming hills behind a storm, or for the deep incense of sweet cedar-resin wood smoke in fresh glittering mists. Nor is there a name for any *one* of the hundreds of shades of gray that reign over winter glimpses of that sometimes forgotten heavenly body, the sun. Such naming is the work of the first speakers, the poets and writers, and the architects of the Northwest.

One of the aims of architecture is to give form to the words of the poets, to respect the meeting of land, water, and sky. The best Northwest architecture could exist nowhere else: it is *of* the terrain and designed to keep it within reach. Embodying the impulses of the Northwest, the architecture speaks to us in a language that has no need for words.

Retreat architecture in the Pacific Northwest is designed for ritual. An early piece of significant Northwest coastal architecture was the house built by Chief Weah, a Haida priest, around 1850. Designed and built to serve as a winter retreat in Massett, British Columbia, it was the largest house in a sweeping beach-front village, where it sat in the center of the community, protected by a copse of totems. First Nation structures were customarily located in unassuming places, similar to the locations we choose for retreats today. They were "hidden in estuaries, on bays, along streams, or on steep bluffs . . . along and immediately above the beaches, opening onto the beach or parallel to the water . . . rarely were they placed well back from water." [4]

Grassy dunes on the Oregon coast.

Views, ambience, and waterfront exposure allowed First Nation communities a measure of vigilance and resourcefulness. Good broad beaches were important for pulling up heavy canoes, as well as for fishing from the shore. More private locations were sometimes chosen for defensive reasons. Carving embellished the totems that safeguarded houses and signaled which gods were in attendance. They also protected the large gatherings and ceremonies that took place inside houses such as Chief Weah's, where Captain George Vancouver and Captain James Cook may have been among the guests. Chief Weah's house was nearly eighty feet in length. "Except for the roof, all integral pieces form part of an interlocking framework and wall structure . . . some parts would be difficult or impossible to remove without dismantling much of the structure." [5]

Chief Weah's builders used twenty-foot peeled logs for vertical corner posts and two posts at the center of the building, three to four feet apart, at each end of the house. The central posts were several feet taller than the corner posts and determined the angle of the roof and the position of the gable. The exterior vertical wallboards were erected, followed by the roof, whose weight stabilized and held the interlocking frame in place. The roof was uniquely constructed. Each cedar plank was carved into a utilitarian U-shape and fitted together in an alternating pattern, one up, one down. This technique formed a seal and created shallow gutters that directed rainwater off the building. Another attractive feature of the roof was its convertibility. In good weather the large planks were lifted and moved aside—creating an early version of the modern skylight—with the aid of a long pole from inside the house, which opened the roof to welcome fresh air and available sunlight.

The interior exemplified what we refer to as loft living: large and open with high interior volumes. Woven cedar screens separated private spaces from public. Furnishings were spare, a mix of simple carved stools, large worktables, and short, movable ladders. There were also some "imported" mid-nineteenth-century wooden English chairs, sometimes with arms. Racks for drying herbs and salmon were suspended by steel chains, which had been traded with Russian sailors. Round, machine-made metal poles, used as ships' railings, were installed on the upper platform as balcony handrails. The commons was an elevated shelf that surrounded the domestic fire pit area, nine feet below entry level. The first shelf—for social events—was four feet above the fire; the second shelf—for privacy—about four feet above that at the level of the main entrance. This arrangement of planned space is perfectly workable for a contemporary house, and a similar mix of minimalist and European furnishings are found in today's Northwest retreats.

The Haida, Nootka, and Chinook all had early contact with Chinese shipbuilders and carpenters. In 1789, London brokers dispatched the ship *Argonaut*, with "29 Chinese artificers" onboard carrying orders to build a permanent post at Nootka Sound, which was already well known in the financial and power centers of England. Chinese builders were skilled in the practice of wooden trabeated construction, in which mortised, bracketed, and interlocking framing systems are clad with lightweight exterior wooden walls. Small ceramic models from the Han period (ca. 202 B.C.–220 A.D.) show that these construction techniques were used as early as the Shang era (ca. 1766–1122 B.C.). Chinese builders had already used the gable roof, with long overhangs and no

Chief Weah's winter retreat on the beach at Massett, British Columbia, ca. 1890.

structural dependence on the walls. The Chinese also built houses with wood and earth, preferring to use stone for bridges and fortified structures. The dates, venture of trading, and structural similarities in construction types indicate that the Chinese craftsmen who were sent to build the large factory for the fur trade and who constructed small boats on the beaches of Nootka Sound disseminated their technical and architectural knowledge to cultures of the Northwest. Their small boats were used in short trading excursions and village-to-village visits up and down a shoreline where everything was traded, including knowledge. Among the Northwest coast styles, that of the Haida was the most architecturally complex, exhibiting the influence of the Chinese craftsmen and commanding enough to have influenced the architecture of the Chinook tribes around the Columbia River.

The legacy of these First Nation peoples gives continuity to the short history of Northwest coast architecture. The character of the region's interior and exterior architecture is still present in a style that insinuated itself into the landscape, featured Asian intricacies and simplicities, and ultimately, due to advances in materials alone, focused on the availability of light. All of these elements could be found in Chief Weah's house, as well as in the work of influential Northwest twentieth-century architects A. E. Doyle, Pietro Belluschi, Roland Terry, Wendell Lovett, and John Storrs.

the architecture of adventure

Mixed foursome at the traditional Scottish links layout at Gearhart, Oregon, the oldest golf course in the Western U.S., 1902 (**TOP LEFT**); *publisher, poet, and Pony Express rider Joaquin Miller writing at campsite at Crater Lake, 1905* (**TOP RIGHT**); *Model A on road blasted from ocean basalt at Hug Point, accessible only during low tide* (**BOTTOM LEFT**); *Mazama rock climber atop the 500-foot Two Needles formation, Wallawa County, Oregon, 1910* (**BOTTOM RIGHT**).

Bathers at Seaside beach, Oregon, 1910 (**TOP**); *Eddie Bauer trout-fishing in a bow tie, 1923* (**BOTTOM**).

IT IS NOT COINCIDENTAL that the numerous early architectural styles in the Northwest are variations, if not exact replicas, of East Coast and European styles. In many cases, families would not be willing to relocate to this unknown and harsh land without the assurances of the status and comforts associated with the houses being left behind. They packed their courage with them, and it often resided in the design of their house. In 1890, for example, the Craigdarrock Castle was built in Seattle to satisfy the Victorian tastes of the wife of coal baron Robert Dunsmuir. In central Oregon, Dorothy Lawson McCall, (wife of Harvard graduate Hal McCall, daughter-in-law to the Massachusetts governor Samuel Walker McCall, daughter of Wall Street's notorious "Copper King," Thomas W. Lawson, and mother of Oregon's future Governor Tom McCall) lived in Westernwold. The ranch was a variation of her father's thousand-acre estate, Dreamwold, in Massachusetts. In Eugene, Oregon, a 7,000-square-foot stone house, heated entirely with geothermal power, was built for a woman who had refused to leave Germany unless she could move into the "same" house. Well-educated architects and those who had apprenticed in the offices of established firms were drawn to the Northwest by the invitations of friends and colleagues, and often by the promise of work, which many times had evaporated by the time they arrived. Washington State, however, with thirty-five registered architects, was given an American Institute of Architects charter in 1894.

At the turn of the century, the Pacific Northwest coast was still an area of wild adventure, although it also offered more cultured varieties of recreation. Joaquin Miller, for example, the controversial poet, journalist, playwright, and Pony Express rider, often camped at

*Illahee, the Lake Washington summer cabin of Seattle judge Thomas Burke and wife Caroline, in 1908 (**TOP LEFT**); rustic furnishings and interior of Illahee (**TOP RIGHT**); a ten-bedroom retreat in the Columbia Gorge called the Farmhouse, designed by A. E. Doyle in 1915 for merchant Julius Meier. The use of enormous peeled logs echo their use in Chief Weah's house sixty years earlier (**BOTTOM LEFT**); 1908 summer retreat on Seattle's Lake Washington (**BOTTOM RIGHT**).*

Harry Wentz studio balcony with view from Neahkahnie mountain over the Pacific, 1916 (**TOP**); *wreck of the* Glenesslin *on the rocks below Harry Wentz studio balcony, ca. 1913* (**BOTTOM**).

Oregon's Crater Lake, following old trails before the first roads were built there in 1905. Pacific beaches were becoming a favorite destination, and newly constructed ocean roads, such as the wild and wet one at Hug Point, allowed courageous souls to drive along the coastline at low tide. Other hearty pursuits included rock and mountain climbing, golf (the first courses in the western United States were laid out in Gearhart, Oregon, in 1902), tennis, rowing, bathing, and bicycling.

Vacation architecture began to flourish just prior to the turn of the century. In Washington, city dwellers headed for the coast, to the many small islands and harbors in Puget Sound, and to surrounding lakes. Houseboats on Lake Washington appeared as early as 1888. In 1898, Seattle judge Thomas Burke and his wife, Caroline, built a summer home, Illahee, on the western shore of Lake Washington. It wasn't reminiscent of a known architectural style, but the large, wraparound porch and the sloping barn-style shed roof reflected simple farm and storage buildings. Built at the edge of the water, its interior was tall, sporting an open paneled ceiling, simple angular trusses, a loft, and a fireplace. The interior appointments were a collection of baskets, blankets, rugs, and simple vacation furniture.

One early architect to arrive in the Northwest was A. E. Doyle, who came from Santa Cruz, California, with his family when he was a boy. As a young man, Doyle took an apprenticeship in the Portland architectural firm of Whidden and Lewis and in 1903 left the firm to attend Columbia University. He subsequently worked in the offices of Henry Bacon, traveled through Europe, and returned to Portland in 1907. Doyle's architectural legacy is far-reaching, with large commercial, institutional,

*Oregon governor Oswald West built his summer cabin above Cannon Beach, ca. 1922 (**TOP LEFT**); a 1991 arson fire almost destroyed the Oswald West summer cabin. Working from historic photos, plans, and site drawings, the cabin was restored (**TOP RIGHT**); original wrought-iron hardware and fixtures were replicated for the Oswald West cabin restoration (**BOTTOM LEFT**); the restored interior of West's log cabin (**BOTTOM RIGHT**).*

The Multnomah Falls Lodge beside the 620-foot drop of the falls. The graceful stone and wood lodge was designed in 1923 by A. E. Doyle.

urban, and residential projects that are today a part of Oregon's prized heritage. Of note here, however, are the subtleties found in a succession of vacation cottages he designed between 1908 and 1916. Doyle's influence is recognizable in the work of a young architect who would become his associate, Pietro Belluschi.

In 1915 and 1916, Doyle designed two summer homes that could not be more different from one another. The first is the Farmhouse, designed for the merchant baron Julius Meier. The ten-bedroom retreat was located on a great bluff in the Columbia Gorge. The house used a peeled-log corner-post structural frame designed much like Chief Weah's house of 1850. The interior living room was a grand, open area measuring thirty feet by forty-six feet by twenty-two feet in height. This house was a pivotal design in that it nodded to the past, to the vernacular architecture of the Northwest Coast. The other home is the 1916 Harry Wentz Studio on Neahkahnie Mountain on the Oregon coast. The design of the Wentz Studio is considered the "most interesting and ... most significant,"[6] in part because it was a collaboration between friends (Wentz and Doyle). The cottage is said to be a source of inspiration for the future of the Northwest Style, as defined by Wentz and Doyle's friend and colleague Pietro Belluschi.

Another of Doyle's everlasting designs is the 1923 stone and wood lodge at Multnomah Falls. Designed in the rustic manner next to Oregon's tallest falls, the lodge offers a perfect view of the 620-foot drop from the upper and lower falls, over pillow lava. The Multnomah Falls Lodge is one of the most visited sites in the state. In an example of the design's exquisite adaptability, the firm of Fletcher, Farr, and Ayotte designed a large, glass-paned

The snow-covered Timberline Lodge on the slopes of Mount Hood, Oregon, in the moonlight, 1945. Ray Atkeson photo (**TOP**); Eleanor Roosevelt's "deluxe parlor bedroom with fireplace." The room is appointed with the lodge's signature handcrafted furnishings, textiles, and original art, which furnish the rooms today (**LOWER LEFT**); the massive central fireplace in the Timberline Lodge ski lobby. The decor features the curved post-and-lintel arches that are found throughout the lodge and in its furnishings (**LOWER RIGHT**).

skylight and outdoor stone patio for the pleasure of lodge guests. (The same firm also accomplished a detailed and beautiful restoration of the Crater Lake Lodge.)

Oswald West, Oregon's governor from 1911 to 1915, built the Cannon Beach summer cottage. West was the first politician to take action for the protection of the 361 miles of Oregon coastline from private ownership and development. His own small cabin sat on the slope toward the beach. Many of the log or timber structures were lost to fire, as was the cabin. Again, Fletcher, Farr, and Ayotte was responsible for the restoration of this summer cottage.

Over at the mountains, the first rumblings for the construction of an overnight ski lodge at Mount Hood were being heard. By the mid-1920s plans were being drawn for a lodge, a ski club, and mountain climbing chalets. A decade later, Gilbert Stanley Underwood became the consulting architect on what became the Timberline project. Forest Service architects drew up the plans, which were influenced by the chateaux and alpine architecture of Europe. In the Northwest, this style was called Cascadian. The construction of Timberline Lodge began in the summer of 1936. The builders consisted of a Works Progress Administration (WPA) workforce of skilled and unskilled crews, and Forest Service supervisors; 10 percent of the workers were non-WPA.

The first snows began in December, and the construction went on. Stonemasons cut boulders and warmed their hands on small stoves while they worked. The exterior walls were constructed, as was the gigantic central stone fireplace that is the focal point of the entire building. Wood carvers, stonemasons, and iron workers began creating signature elements for the interior that are repeated throughout the lodge, such as the curved post-and-lintel arch, which appears in furniture and doorways.

Marjorie Hoffman Smith, who had been a professional interior designer in Portland since 1929, was hired as the interior designer and furnishings coordinator and managed the work as a Federal Arts Project (FAP), the fine arts division of the WPA. Smith was the daughter of the Boston painter, photographer, and philanthropist Julia Hoffman. The Hoffman family moved in 1905 from Boston to Portland where they founded the Portland Arts and Crafts Society and also sponsored the first class of the Portland Museum Art School. In her work on Timberline Lodge, Smith organized the serious, well-trained painters, sculptors, metalsmiths, glass workers, and weavers; everything was to be made by hand. This included the furniture, andirons, boot scrapers, chandeliers, upholstery, beds, lamps, rugs, watercolor paintings, gates, and the fittings for all exterior and interior doors of the forty-nine guest rooms, dining rooms, and dormitories.

The dedication of Timberline Lodge took place over national radio on September 19, 1937, when President and Eleanor Roosevelt visited Mount Hood. In 1944, Marjorie Hoffman Smith wrote about the project:

The job was to be done and done in a hurry…there was no time for blueprinting. Creative outlets were offered to some who had long been deprived of the privilege—and to others who had never experienced them.…The response was one of the most stimulating of human adventures. Workmen left with tears in their eyes; and not one, but many, look back at it as the most interesting work experience in their lives.[7]

While the Forest Service architects of Timberline Lodge dug deep into tradition, the new architecture was

*The Andrew Kerr beach house at Gearhart. The crest of dunes facing the ocean (**TOP**); the peeled log pole at entry is reminiscent of pole at the Wentz cabin at Neahkahnie (**BOTTOM**).*

appearing. Pietro Belluschi, a new, young apprentice in A. E. Doyle's office who was later to become his partner, was perhaps the greatest gift to ever migrate to the Pacific Northwest. A lover of the environment, Belluschi came to the United States as an exchange student to Cornell University after receiving a doctorate in engineering at the University of Rome in 1922. He began work with Doyle in 1925. When he arrived, Belluschi saw strong evidence of the emerging International Style in Portland. He also noticed that a sensibility for the local traditions and culture—a "regionalist sensibility"—was taking hold. Doyle, Belluschi, and John Yeon were the first to be associated with an emerging style identified with northwest architecture. Architecture was, for them, an attempt to solve the problems of human nature in a new, modern world. Their focus was interior spaces that with human presence exuded a moral and ethical vitality that helped meet the needs of modern life.

One of Belluschi's own favorites is the 1941 Peter Kerr vacation home in Gearhart on the Oregon coast. The board-and-batten structure sits on a grassy knoll above the ocean. A peeled log used as a column at the entry is an echo of Doyle's 1916 Wentz Studio at Neahkahnie. Floor-to-ceiling windows faced the Pacific and absorbed the full afternoon sun.

In 1950, Belluschi became Dean of the School of Architecture at M.I.T. He returned to Portland in 1965. While Belluschi was away from the Northwest, his influences were being incorporated into the work of new generations of architects. In Washington State, the voices favoring the Northwest residential idiom were those of Roland Terry, Paul Hayden Kirk, and Wendell Lovett. In Oregon, the rising stars were John Storrs and Van Evera Bailey in the 1950s and 1960s. The next generation was beginning designs that would appear later, in the 1970s.

PURVIS BEACH PLACE

1950

LEA, PEARSON & RICHARDS, ARCHITECT

HENDERSON BAY, PUGET SOUND

In 1950 Jim Purvis, a general contractor in Tacoma, Washington, built a sprawling glass-and-cedar beach place on Henderson Bay in Puget Sound, near Gig Harbor. On Friday afternoons, a short drive across the Narrows Bridge left city days behind. The road led to Wauna, Washington. The weekend meant lots of friends and steaks on the fire, while waterskiing and a continual flurry of activity went on until Monday morning. Purvis used the classic California flooring, red cement, throughout the house; it flowed out to the terrace and down the steps to the pool. Separated from the large living room and fireplace by an open counter and bar, the kitchen was an open workspace with a high ceiling. Eileen Purvis always had a prime rib ready on the Farberware rotisserie for the seemingly endless stream of weekend guests.

A hairpin turn from the main road onto a winding gravel drive down to the shore finds this low, long, and sleek design soaking up the morning sun on the shore of Puget Sound's Henderson Bay (**TOP**); *swimming is a favorite pastime* (**BOTTOM**).

ROLAND TERRY RETREAT

1950

ROLAND TERRY, ARCHITECT

SAN JUAN ISLANDS

One of the main considerations in designing for the Northwest is proper siting. This house, designed and built by architect Roland Terry for himself, is so beautifully grounded in its site, it seems to have been *born* there. Terry made sure that the site was left undisturbed and that no trees were cut. He modified his original design until it allowed for this.

Terry's use of materials creates a complex and refined collage that expresses his unique vision. Here we see the use of seventeen large, peeled posts, echoing those used by Chief Weah's builders one hundred years earlier. Terry used driftwood, reclaimed wood panels, stone, and aggregate concrete with tile mosaics to create refined interiors and elegant exteriors. He cultivated wisteria vines up the exterior walls of the house, between nine-foot shuttered French doors. There, the vines met the sod and wildflower planted roof, which was Terry's emphatic comment about the house and its place in its natural setting. The resulting interior polish and exterior finesse demonstrates a frugality of natural resources that is a model for residential construction.

Architect Roland Terry designed this quintessential northwest retreat in the San Juan Islands. Terry salvaged the oversized driftwood logs and used them with a mix of neo-Regence paneling, sod-roofing, glass walls, and concrete floors in his island cabin (**TOP**); *the double-Dutch, French shuttered doors are an outside entry to the kitchen* (**BOTTOM**).

Terry finessed elegance from simple objects: the concrete aggregate floor features a mosaic of tidal waves that flow through the hall, the living room, and outside to the terrace (**TOP LEFT**); dining or sitting around a fire near the ancient, gnarled cypress is a perfect way to enjoy the beauty of Terry's creation (**TOP RIGHT**); the living room features enormous peeled driftwood logs that Terry found over time and used with glass walls and eclectic furnishings. Terry built the cabin without cutting any trees at all (**BOTTOM**).

NEAHKAHNIE MOUNTAIN BEACH HOUSE

1962

JOHN STORRS, ARCHITECT

JOHN DiMAIO, PHOTOGRAPHER

NEAHKAHNIE, OREGON

*John Storrs sited the beach cabin tightly into the cliff (**LEFT**); the deck with a view to the south for whale watching (**CENTER**); the interior fireplace (**RIGHT**).*

The next best thing to designing and building your own dream house is to find a classic that has been almost forgotten. It is like finding an old Chris Craft on blocks in a garage. Two young architects discovered this cottage several years ago. The house was empty and nearly abandoned. James and Kathleen Meyer fell in love with it and now plan to spend their time restoring what turned out to be an early John Storrs masterpiece. Built in 1962, the house is as perfectly sited as a Puffin nest. "When I drive onto the beach road, I feel my city-skin just floating away.

This house is my therapy. I come here and chip blue tile from the hearth," says James. He and Kathleen found the original plans in the house. Storrs's notes are a text from another era. "It would require two pages of specifications today," said James of the instructions for building the fireplace. Storrs had written simply, "Corbel brick back as fast as possible." James and his own young firm, Opsis, work with earnest to achieve that sort of easy understanding with their contractors.

SALISHAN SPIT RETREAT

1972

RON TRAVERS, ARCHITECT

GLENEDEN BEACH, OREGON

In the Pacific Northwest, people go to the coast in the winter to watch the storms and in the summer to walk on the beach between showers. Ron Travers of Travers/ Johnson Architects designed this retreat at Salishan Spit at Gleneden Beach, Oregon, in 1972. The design respects the climate and uses its own forms to mitigate the unpredictability of the weather. The house sits on a spit of land between the Pacific Ocean and Siletz Bay, overlooking dunes, pines, and native grasses. The main lodge area is an octagon, equipped with a kitchen, fireplace, and lounge; separate bedroom cabins are hexagons built around a courtyard. This design makes views available from many vantages and allows easy movement between buildings. Wind protection is created by glass enclosures around the central courtyard. The circular compound shelters the courtyard, which is terraced around a fire spit. It is a remarkably calm, quiet, and temperate area, with a subtle flow of fresh air over the pitched roof planes above. The house was designed with the friends, families, and clients of the firm in mind, for a bracing seaside escape.

*The view of the lodge and sleeping module from the driftwood-strewn beach (**TOP**); sleeping modules from over the dune (**CENTER**); the central courtyard (**BOTTOM**).*

WASP PASSAGE

1972

WENDELL LOVETT, FAIA

CRANE ISLAND, SAN JUAN ISLANDS

This is the very first retreat that Wendell H. Lovett, FAIA, designed for his family. Located on Wasp Passage on ferry-less Crane Island in the San Juans, the cabin, built in 1972, fits so completely into its setting that it is nearly camouflaged by shadows, sunlight, and shade above the low bank beach. The cabin is a mere twelve feet wide and contains a first floor "living" area, a compact kitchen and bath, and an upper sleeping loft; the cabin has room enough for six close friends. The innovative design uses inverted trusses to cantilever almost twenty feet out over the rocks above the high water line. The trusses support the roof and create framing for the sun deck. The deck is built around the existing trees. This classic Northwest haven was the summer idyll for the architect and his family, and although it is no longer in the family, Wendell has the fondest affection for Wasp Passage and would love to return to it.

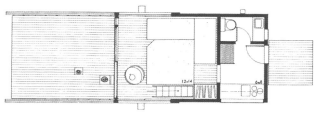

*Designed to house six for the weekend, the cabin appears to float above rocks and shore (**TOP**); the interior offers all the niceties for weekends away, but as summer days are long most time is spent outside (**BOTTOM**).*

SOAPSTONE

1970

WILL MARTIN, ARCHITECT

SOAPSTONE CREEK, OREGON

Model of Soapstone cabin and bridge (**LEFT**); *the cabin being built during early spring* (**CENTER**); *detail of entry gate* (**RIGHT**).

Soapstone was built on twenty-four acres of land located ten miles inland from the Oregon coast, near the confluence of two fresh water creeks fed by a spring water lake. The combined streams flow as one for a quarter mile through the length of the property. The site is heavily wooded with Red Alder, Hemlock, Douglas Fir, and Cedar. The stream is a spawning ground for annual salmon runs. Martin's plan for Soapstone was to provide himself, his wife, and two children with a self-contained environment as an escape from the "conveniences" of the city. The project was to be built entirely by hand (no power tools) by the architect and his carpenter father. This puzzled Will's father, who could not understand why the son, who had achieved a certain amount of success, wished to re-create what had seemed like a struggle

for survival back on their farm in Missouri. Will often thought of having grown up without electricity, telephones, natural gas, heating oil, or food preservatives, as "hard, simple, rewarding, and very beautiful." It was the source of his fierce self-reliance.

> *If thou art worn and hard beset with*
> *sorrows thou wouldst forget, if thou wouldst read a*
> *lesson that will*
> *keep, go to the woods and hills. No*
> *tears dim the sweet look that Nature*
> *wears.*
>
> —Henry Wadsworth Longfellow
> (*recorded in Will Martin's journa*l)

beachcomb for a better tomorrow

WHEN PEOPLE IN NEW YORK say, "We're going to the 'coast,'" they usually mean they're going to the West Coast—Los Angeles or Hollywood perhaps. When people in the Pacific Northwest say, "We're going to the coast," they have in mind only one thing: the narrow slip of geology and geography between the westernmost foothills of the coastal mountain range and the gray-green breakers of the Pacific Ocean. For them, it's not the coast if you can't hear the breakers and smell the salt air. And once at the coast, you need only to cross the beach strewn with sand dollars, scallop shells, gulls' feathers, and, if you're lucky, agates the color of your eyes to dip your bare feet in the surf.

WENTZ / BELLUSCHI
BEACH STUDIO

OWNERS: Peter and Sue Belluschi
ARCHITECT: A. E. Doyle
PHOTOGRAPHER: JOHN DiMAIO

The cabin built for painter Harry Wentz sits on a bluff high above the beach. A mountain stream flows under the footbridge beside the cabin and plunges to the ocean below (**OPPOSITE**); *Except for a skylight added by a former owner, the restoration by Peter and Sue Belluschi returned this architectural treasure to its original state* (**ABOVE**).

A SMALL BEACH COMMUNITY on the Oregon coast, Neahkahnie began as a gathering place for artists and intellectuals in the early part of the twentieth century. The town has also served as an "incubator" for the development of a regional architecture that has become known as the Northwest Style. One of the most significant early cottages in the area is built on a high nib of Neahkahnie Mountain, a site offering an abundance of coastal views to the north and south. Morning mists dissolve as the sun comes up over the Coast Range to the east of the cabin; later, one can settle down to watch a Pacific sunset. The architecture of the cottage was a collaboration between two friends, Harry Wentz, the founder and director of the

Portland Museum Art School, and the architect A. E. Doyle. Their 1916 design embodies Wentz's spirited emotional and artistic dedication to the natural landscape, as well as Doyle's willingness to focus on the inherent aspects of design attributable to the *genius loci*; what the Tillamook Indians called "the spirit of the mountain." Neahkahnie was believed to be a sacred place, and its unique atmosphere was thought to infuse the rocks, trees, and water with a special emotion. Such ideas were congenial to Wentz. Once virtually engulfed in evergreens, the cabin was thus safeguarded from winter storms. The remaining trees are wind-scarred and bent, but the cottage itself ascends to the prevailing light as willingly and as delicately as a trillium.

As a youth, Peter Belluschi spent many summers at this studio with "Uncle Harry" (Wentz). His first vivid memory of Wentz was watching him run up and over the meadow to greet Peter's father, the architect Pietro Belluschi, as they drove up in Pietro's Pierce Arrow. The sweet smell of Wentz's pipe and cedar-wood smoke still mingle with Peter's memories. He recalls a fire always going and spectacular sunsets when herds of deer and elk could be seen bedding down in the fading light. Pietro Belluschi admired the studio's subtle magnificence and declared that "it has function, appropriateness, harmony, materials, setting, orientation; it is modern, emotional and beautiful."[8]

From the bridge, the studio is entered through the front door at the right of the stone chimney. The studio occupies the western portion of the cabin, ending at the small balcony.

*The original handwritten invoice showing construction and material costs for the "Studio Neahkahnie." The total was $1,050, although the contractor haggled with Wentz for another $44 for brass fittings (**LEFT**); studio interior, ca. 1923—the table is now used in the kitchen as the breakfast table (**RIGHT**).*

Peter and Sue Belluschi bought the cottage in 1988, following years of gentle pursuit, and have meticulously preserved both the structure and its furnishings. The studio or great room occupies two-thirds of the main floor on the ocean side. French doors open onto a small balcony with western exposure, while the south wall contains a massive stone fireplace. The northern wall features the innovative use of first-floor oriel windows for natural light. The couches and coffee table were based on drawings by the elder Belluschi. On the cabin's east side, the kitchen and a small guest room and bath face the mountains. A simple stairway leads to the main sleeping area in the loft above the open, spruce-clad studio.

The Belluschis have affectionately restored the cottage and replanted the hillside to capture its original charm. Paintings by Harry Wentz, his students, and friends live harmoniously beside Peter's collection of antique tribal baskets and treasures from the beach.

*Studio interior, ca. 2002—the table was used by Harry Wentz as his painting and work table and the chairs are restored cabin originals (**TOP LEFT**); heirloom furniture and artwork by the Runquist brothers, who were students of Wentz's and lived in the cabin for several years (**TOP RIGHT**); collection of Native American baskets (**BOTTOM**).*

*The view looking up the windswept cliff at the cabin (**ABOVE**); the restored fireplace and hearth—the Japanese wood basket is still used at the fireplace (**OPPOSITE**).*

NEAHKAHNIE HOUSE
AND DIAMOND COTTAGE

OWNERS: Lena Lencek and Gideon Bosker
PHOTOGRAPHER: JOHN DIMAIO

*The Diamond Cottage in Manzanita (**OPPOSITE**); the warm and welcoming sun room of the tiny Diamond Cottage is a perfect spot for reading and relaxing (**ABOVE**).*

FEW KNOW THE BEACH as well as Lena Lencek and Gideon Bosker. The many books the two have written about the pleasures and magnetism of the beach are informative and evocative. The couple was drawn to these cottages in Manzanita, and to neighboring Neahkahnie, by their 1980s work on the history of Portland architecture. While researching architect A. E. Doyle's projects, they visited his cottages in Neahkahnie and were immediately enchanted by their magical location in the shadow of the mountain. The sea birds skimming the waves at sunset, the changing landscape of the beach (narrow and sharp in the winter, wide and flat in the summer when tide pools are broad and shallow enough to fill with warm

35

A few quiet hours next to the wood stove with a cup of tea and a good book is worth the trip to the beach.

water for a brief swim), the profusion of starfish piled up on the rocks at low tide—all of these were more than enough to draw the couple to the area. They were also stirred by Harry Wentz's expeditions to the coast in the teens to paint the virgin landscape, and by Pietro Belluschi's stories of coming west as a young immigrant, confronting the sublime landscape, and the terror he felt when he stood on the sharp promontory on which the Wentz cottage perches. And then there was also the poetry inherent in the site for both Lena and Gideon. Each had grown up on the edge of sea: she on the Adriatic, he on the Mediterranean. They discovered that this area has everything one needs for paradise: mountain, forest, ocean, river, delta. There is the beach, the quiet inlets with nesting cranes, eagles, and coots. There is berry picking, mushrooming, crabbing, and horseback riding across the dunes.

The Neahkahnie house was built in the late thirties as a lookout point from which the Coast Guard kept watch over the horizon for enemy subs and ships during World War II. Diamond Cottage was built in the teens and was restored by a "hippie" builder who slathered it in no fewer than six varieties of scrap lumber and windows scavenged from a variety of demolition jobs. Lena and Gideon pulled it all together, and Lena is vastly proud of the kitchen, which she designed. As the beloved Neahkahnie house is just a little too small to hold extended family and guests, when the opportunity came to buy Diamond Cottage, Lena and Gideon decided to make it into their guest house. About a mile down the beach, it offers their guests the gift of privacy.

*A deck hammock is often most convenient (**TOP**); knotty pine paneling, French doors, and fir floors make a cozy dining area more spacious (**BOTTOM LEFT**); the writing desk at the window (**BOTTOM RIGHT**).*

The former Coast Guard cabin's retrofitted windows, formerly used to search the seas for vessels in trouble, now serve as a source of inspiration (LEFT); the kitchen conveys the owner's affection for her cookie jar collection (TOP RIGHT); a small yard offers large shrubs, rosemary, and heather (BOTTOM RIGHT); Neahkahnie cottage was turned into a Royere-by-the-Sea bungalow in a fantasia of organic shapes, fabrics, and mid-century furniture (OPPOSITE).

BOLES BEACH RETREAT

ARCHITECT: Stanley Boles, FAIA

OWNERS: Stanley Boles and Wendy Kahle

PHOTOGRAPHER: LAURIE BLACK

Beyond the trees, the stone path leads to a courtyard and the weekend getaway (**OPPOSITE**); *the Boles's sleek and serene living area* (**ABOVE**).

PORTLAND ARCHITECT STANLEY BOLES created this tranquil weekend retreat in the Oregon coastal community of Neskowin. The natural materials he used, as well as the transparency of the design, allow the structure to blend into the narrow, forested in-fill site. A stone walk leading to the house serves as a meditative path beneath a canopy of firs, moss, and boulders, culminating in a tiny moss and stone courtyard at the entry of the Boles's three-story beach house, a quiet counterpoint to the crashing breakers to the west.

The first two levels contain Wendy's studio, where she is currently working on large-scale still-life drawings of domestic items like clothing, shoes, and handbags.

The second level also houses compact and genial guest accommodations, which can be secluded by sliding partitions. Additional sliding wall panels and doors of opaque glass allow interior spaces a flow-through translucency while providing additional privacy for the bedroom and bath spaces. The crowning floor of this sanctuary foregoes the anticipated open-beam ceiling for a trim, flush one, giving added dimension to the free flow of the living, dining, and food-preparation areas. Floor-to-ceiling windows in the main living space expand the sense of openness while framing ample ocean views. French doors on each side of the living area open onto small terraces.

The stone path to the entry is lined with moss and ferns (OPPOSITE); *craft and wood create an atmosphere of tranquility* (ABOVE); *the site and floor plan for a small parcel of land* (RIGHT).

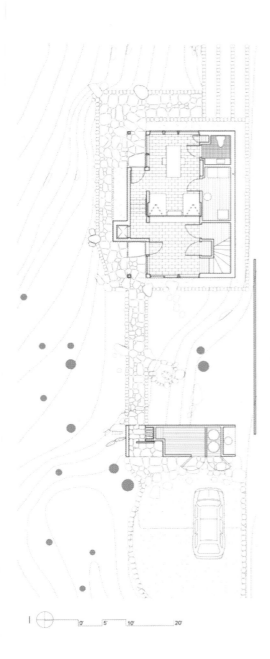

The elegantly appointed living room has one small "wall" that houses the fireplace, wood storage, and media cabinets within the larger glass wall on the south face of the house (**ABOVE**); *the living room and ocean beyond* (**OPPOSITE**).

The east balcony allows one to look directly into lichen- and moss-covered branches and enjoy the indelible scents of cedar-infused ocean air over a loamy courtyard. The west French doors open onto a balcony from which the sound of the ocean and the rustle of the treetops is heard. To invoke the liberating qualities of a weekend out-of-doors, Boles made the fireplace a focal point in the midst of the gardens, wilderness, and ocean seen beyond the windows. The slender and dramatic profile of this retreat in the evening light offers ample evidence of the magnificence and grace of thoughtful design.

*The daylight view shows the compact in-fill site and the limit of the design footprint (**OPPOSITE**); the entry foyer at courtyard level (**ABOVE LEFT**); guest quarters on the other side of entry. Wood panels close for complete privacy (**ABOVE RIGHT**).*

LONG BEACH HOUSE

ARCHITECT: Replinger Hossner
DESIGN TEAM: Jim Replinger, Tim Hossner,
Christopher Osolin
INTERIOR DESIGN: Rocky Rochon Design
PHOTOGRAPHER: MICHAEL MOORE

Dusk and grassy dunes on the Washington coast (**OPPOSITE**)*;
along the colonnade, steps disappear into the sand* (**ABOVE**)*.*

AFTER FALLING IN LOVE with the silence of long, solitary stretches of dunes and grass, a Seattle couple decided to build a retreat on the Long Beach Peninsula, near Willapa Bay, on the southern Washington coast. Days away from the city are spent with their two young children in this distinctive ocean setting, where the family enjoys the flight patterns and landings of migratory birds, the sweeping and changing beachscapes, and of course, the coastal weather. Their three-acre seascape is a delicate natural habitat, and the design of the house conscientiously refrains from intrusion into the dunes. To preserve and enjoy the ridge of eelgrass and dunes, the house was built two hundred feet from the high tide shoreline.

A vivacious combination of style, purpose, and delight, the house's charm begins inside, where playfulness and inspiration await child, teen, and adult. A visit to the kitchen, for example, offers a first glimpse of magic. Glass ceiling tiles may appear to be placed in a random pattern. They are, however, situated as Mintaka, Alnilam, Alnitak, Rigel, and Bellatrix, the brightest stars in the constellation Orion. On the other side of the ceiling, the shining lights perforate the floor in the children's loft, creating an illuminated map of the entire constellation. Another entertaining feature is the hand-crank cable system, designed to ferry notes, toys, and surprises from one end of the U-shaped loft to another. A rescued blackboard forms one of the walls in the children's loft, which is decorated with artwork, doodles, and messages. Hinged bookshelves, disappearing beds, peekaboo openings, and a crow's nest all add to the pleasure of being at the beach.

The house is designed as a large central cabin, from which narrow hallways lead to private, detached sleeping quarters at either end. The main section of the house con-

*The children's sleeping area (**LEFT**); a fun way to pass messages (**CENTER**); the children's loft, where the shape of Orion shines through the glass floor tiles from the lights in the kitchen below (**RIGHT**); the living room with the children's loft above, the crow's nest at the end of the loft, and the kitchen area below the loft (**OPPOSITE**).*

tains the entry, kitchen, dining, and living areas, each delineated by subtle use of stairs and slight dais appointments, ceiling heights, and cabinetwork. The owners' choice of furnishings and art reveals a stylish sensibility alongside their whimsicality.

The design follows through to the outside spaces, which are equally marvelous and where gatherings on the terrace often take place. A large part of being at the beach is spending time out-of-doors in every sort of weather. This carefully conceived exterior is composed of a series of spaces easily converted to "rooms." Two sixteen-by-twenty-foot courts on the ocean side of the main building are enclosed by walls on three sides, opening toward the dunes and the ocean. The courts, which are linked to a long, open colonnade, become enclosed private spaces through the use of large, rolling shutters that are similar to old warehouse or barn doors. They offer a perfect solution for either screened privacy or protection from the wind. Clearly, the owners worked with their architect to design the setting for a lifetime of cherished adventures and memorable days and nights. The steps disappear into the sand. This is a home of engaged appropriateness and convenience, with an immeasurable knack for knowing what it means to get away.

Loft Level

1. Loft
2. Guest
3. Reading
4. Bunkroom Loft

Main Level

1. Entry
2. Living/Dining
3. Kitchen
4. Bath
5. Bedroom
6. Bunkroom
7. Garage
8. Court

0   16'

The living room, designed for casual recreation and relaxation in front of the fireplace (ABOVE); the floor plan showing the central living area and two sleeping cabins at either end of the main structure and a bunk room behind it (LEFT); the exterior fireplace on the colonnade between patio courts (OPPOSITE).

The open kitchen plan steps down into living area (OPPOSITE); the crow's nest with trapdoor and surrounding views (LEFT); views from the crow's nest (BELOW).

One of the two courts along the colonnade between the central living/dining area and the sleeping areas (**ABOVE**); *the vast expanse of sand dunes and grass between the retreat and the beach* (**OPPOSITE**).

TAHMAHNAWIS
AT DEVIL'S LAKE

OWNERS: Dan and Kathy Harmon

ARCHITECT: GBD Architects

DESIGN TEAM: Alan Beard, FAIA, Gene Callan,
Craig Stockbridge

PHOTOGRAPHER: MICHAEL MATHERS

BOTH A NOUN AND AN ADJECTIVE, *tahmahnawis* is a word borrowed from early-nineteenth-century Chinook jargon (a mixture of French, English, northwest coast Native American dialects, and Russian) meaning "spirited place." The myth of Devil's Lake tells the story of a young Tillamook Indian girl who slipped a canoe into the water one night and became disoriented in the darkness. She was pulled far below the surface of the water by the devil, who took the form of an octopus. Entangled in his tentacles, she was carried out to sea and lost. Today a sense of mystery still lingers over the legendary lake (it is, in actuality, connected to the ocean by an underground channel) that surrounds this contemporary lodge on the tip of an isolated peninsula.

Night view of Devil's Lake from Tahmahnawis
(**OPPOSITE**); Tahmahnawis *sits on a peninsula*
reaching far into Devil's Lake (**ABOVE**).

Sketch of entry loggia (LEFT); interior detail of entry loggia (CENTER); the stone and bronze gatepost (RIGHT); the sitting room with cut stone fireplace and the lake beyond (OPPOSITE).

Few homes possess the level of craftsmanship found in the construction and detailing of *Tahmahnawis*. This should not be surprising, as the owner Dan Harmon is vice president of one of the country's major construction companies. When he was a child, his family had a summer home on a lake near Spokane, Washington. As an adult, Dan wanted to replicate family gatherings in his own vacation home in a lodge atmosphere with bright, open interiors, outdoor fireplaces and terraces, and private loft enclaves. Every detail was presented in forty-nine sheets of drawings before the project was handed over to the general contractor. The forms and craftsmanship at *Tahmahnawis* were inspired by the early twentieth-century work of Gilbert Stanley Underwood, a man who defined lodge architecture with Yosemite's Ahwahnee

Hotel and Oregon's Timberline Lodge on the slopes of Mount Hood. *Tahmahnawis* was designed to keep guests engaged in the enchantments of lakeside recreation, social vignettes, and sunsets over the lake seen through the dark green and blue mosaic of two-hundred-foot-tall fir trees against the soft-toned skies.

Large, covered exterior spaces accommodate informal outdoor gatherings. The tree-lined approach leads to an elegant entry loggia, where the strength of lodge design is unmistakable. A gentle, sloping roof floats on timber trusses and beams, which rest on massive stone pillars. The themes of this bold yet simple structure are repeated throughout the house and guest quarters.

The front entry opens directly into the great room, where textures and elevations are illuminated through

windows that span the height and width of the west end of the room, admitting direct sunlight and dancing reflections from the surface of the lake. A bar, built of local Tenino stone and capped with salvaged vertical-grain fir, separates the sitting room from a quietly recessed living room. A custom-crafted open stair made of slabs of salvaged timber leads to second-floor bedrooms and an upper-level loft that looks out over the lake.

The lodge's design and construction make use of reclaimed, certified, and engineered materials. Douglas fir timbers from a six-hundred-year-old tree were reclaimed from the old Terminal 2 on the Willamette River and used not only for their strength and beauty, but also to set the standard for all of the materials used in the construction. Native materials, including Tenino sandstone; certified materials like red cedar, mahogany, and cherry woods; and composite sheathing, roof panels, and microlaminates all express the fact that the conservation of resources was a high priority.

The site lies between pristine wetlands and Devil's Lake. Out of respect for the wetlands and the woodland at its edge—which included a five-hundred-year-old giant sequoia, and native Aspen and Douglas firs—site preservation was a primary concern. Only one tree on the site was lost. The house fulfills the desire of its owners for both enjoyment and privacy, and together they created a place that their family will cherish for generations to come.

*The stone, wood, and steel staircase designed by Craig Stockbridge features steps made of four-inch-by-four-foot pieces of 600-year-old recycled Douglas fir (*OPPOSITE*); the living room is off the main entry and shares the large windows with the sitting room (*TOP RIGHT*); the kitchen and dining areas feature soft wood and hand-crafted light fixtures (*BOTTOM RIGHT*).*

up north

THE 172 ISLANDS OF THE SAN JUANS, with their rocky shorelines and forested ridges, form an archipelago in the straits between Canada's Vancouver Island and the northwest coast of Washington. Named by Spanish explorers around 1790, the islands attracted members of the counter culture of the 1960s and '70s, and permanent residents are likely to have learned a protest song or two back in the old days. The larger islands—among them Orcas, Shaw, Lopez, and San Juan—are linked by Washington State ferries, but some of the islands are so tiny and hidden that they can be reached only by private seaplane or boat. An outing or a commute on the ferry is a splendid experience, as bald eagles drift overhead and a pod of orcas swims in the water below.

HOUSE ON THE ROCKS

ARCHITECT: Daly, Genik; Chris Genik, principal
PHOTOGRAPHER: JOHN DiMAIO

This retreat looks like it was built elsewhere and later set into this garden of boulders (**OPPOSITE**); *the retreat viewed from down the slope* (**ABOVE**).

UPON SEEING THE "BOULDER HOUSE" for the first time, one could easily imagine that its occupant is someone who really loves rocks. It may be just a coincidence, but one of the owners is, in fact, a geologist. Indeed this rough terrain (where fifty-four tons of metamorphic rock can be yours for the cost of moving it), with its glacier-polished granite and lively seismic zone, offers a beautiful setting for this geologist's dream house.

In order to accommodate the owners' wish to leave eighty-foot-tall cedars, stands of white maple, *arbutus*, and mature spruce and granite outcroppings undisturbed, the design was separated into three wings. The cluster of wings enfolds an entry court, which leads from the escarpment by stairs and a stone pathway to a bridge.

The kitchen components seem to float above the floors (LEFT); the fireplace is the focus of the living area (RIGHT); the hearth side of the fire-place faces the living area, the desk level side faces the common space, and the bench side faces the view out the windows (OPPOSITE).

The upper level hall and gallery. The engineered wood ceiling beams show the seam where the roof design begins its butterfly angle (**OPPOSITE**); a worm's-eye view of the wood treatment on the stairs (**ABOVE**).

The bridge's railing is set at an angle to maintain a sense of openness as the courtyard entry passes through one of the major outcrops. The materials surrounding the courtyard are solid yet warm and welcoming, a lovely reflection of the ruggedness of the site and the comforts within.

The living room wing is given warmth by the wood used in the cabinets, stairs, and wall cladding. Other woodworking details include the front door designed and crafted by a local boatbuilder, and the floor, which is composed of resawn eight-inch first-growth fir planking reclaimed from an old aircraft hanger. Adding to the overall attractiveness is the engineered wood in the sixteen-by-two-and-a-half-inch ceiling beams of timber strand and resin.

The strongest interior element is the sculptural fireplace, a signature design for architect Chris Genik. The fireplace performs several functions several ways. As an ordinary fireplace, its extensions cantilever into the living and dining areas, helping to regulate room temperatures. It is also a spatial divider, forming more intimate spaces within the larger interior volume. It is a functional furniture component: a warming bench on one side, a desk or work surface on another. This multipurpose design introduces the fireplace as the focal point of the living space, yet allows for easy movement around it.

The bedrooms are located on the upper level. The framing has the shape of an inverted boat hull, and its soft curvature creates a gently bowed fanning of the rooflines. The delicacy associated with a butterfly-wing roof dramatizes the contrast between the massive boulders and their intricate relationship with the house.

SEMIAHMOO RETREAT

ARCHITECT: Finne Architects; Nils C. Finne, FAIA

PHOTOGRAPHER: ART GRICE

*The entryway leads to a sun-filled landing off the terrace (**OPPO-
SITE**); a freehand sketch of Semiahmoo by Nils Finne (**ABOVE**).*

PRIOR TO DISCUSSING this new home at the Semiahmoo
Resort on the Canada-U.S. border, the owners had lived
in one house for thirty years and were new to the idea of
working with an architect. They had some ideas about
what they hoped to incorporate into the house, and architect Nils Finne patiently collaborated with them. The
results surprised them, as they were off in a new, modern
direction. Finne, a designer who trusts the collaborative
design process, moved confidently forward. He realized
from the beginning that the key to comprehending this
project was to tie the idea of the design to a language that
was familiar to the clients. That language became deci-
pherable through the materials they wanted to live with:

A detail of the door, showing hardware designed as a symbol of the owner's career in aerospace (**ABOVE LEFT**); *interior stair detail* (**ABOVE RIGHT**); *the outdoor terrace between living, dining, and sleeping areas of the house* (**OPPOSITE**).

granite, cherry wood, copper, cedar. In addition, a highly detailed level of craftsmanship was required to achieve a quality that had been a part of their beloved older home. Finne worked diligently to design furnishings, details, and other features that would evoke events and memories meaningful to the owners, as well as stand alone as elegant objects in and of themselves.

The house works on several architectural themes. First, it can be seen as a fragment of the larger natural order. There were also subtle adaptations of modernism to the idea of craft in building. Finally, the project can be seen as an investigation of the emotive qualities. Style makes its claim and expresses its own sense of what matters. This is particularly true of the use of stone, wood, and natural light.

The site slopes westward to the protected water of Semiahmoo Bay. The base of the house is a plinth of split-faced Canada granite, twelve inches above grade on the uphill side, graduating to a full story downhill. Atop the rough stone is a series of Douglas fir fan trusses on steel-banded fir columns, which lift and distance the roof system from the enclosure walls. The angle of the roofing plane results in a continuous clerestory band of fir-framed windows and v-groove cedar panels, while high clerestory windows provide natural light and ventilation throughout the house. In general, fewer trees are harvested on Finne's projects, and large timbers are frequently conserved by his use of banded wood columns and beams composed of smaller pieces.

The main living level is upstairs, where an outdoor terrace is carved into the building just outside the entry hall, separating the living area from the master bedroom. Both upper wings enjoy the ever-changing and beguiling views, glorious late afternoon angles of the sun, and evening sunsets on the west bay and beyond. Guest rooms and a large entertainment area are located on the lower level, within the stone plinth.

The Semiahmoo retreat is filled with custom mill-work and cabinetry designed for many individual spaces. Laser equipment was used to create copper light fixtures and cherry wood furniture with inlay, all designed by Finne. Interior stonework, etched glass, and stair details are a vocabulary that is intuitively understood. After a year of design and two years of construction, Nils Finne's clients have learned the language of modernism well.

The main living area showing the clerestory and the architect's use of banded laminate wood. Hanging copper light shades designed by the architect were laser cut (**OPPOSITE**); a view of the living and dining areas from the kitchen. The kitchen area is camouflaged by glass screens with a bead-blasted design that recurs in the furniture (**ABOVE**).

The delicate wood and steel staircase allows the free-flow of sunlight in many directions (**LEFT**); *a custom-built bed echoes the glass design in the kitchen* (**RIGHT**); *sunlight floods the upstairs bedrooms through clerestory windows* (**OPPOSITE**).

TERRA BELLA RETREAT

(WHIDBEY ISLAND RETREAT)

OWNER: Linda Beeman

ARCHITECT: DeForest Ogden Design Office

**PHOTOGRAPHERS: JOHN DIMAIO, STEVE KEATING,
JOHN DEFOREST**

*The entry of this hidden retreat and gallery. The owner specified
"no cedar shingles and no river-rock trim." Fiber-cement siding
with stained wood trim was used (**OPPOSITE**); a niche of nature-
sustaining craft (**ABOVE**).*

WHEN ARCHITECTS ARE INTRIGUED by a woodland
site, its pathways, and nesting hollows, the thresholds and
gradual changes in vegetation, the clearings and shadows
that follow the course of the sun and of storms, it is certain that every detail of design will be investigated. This
small house and gallery, Terra Bella, by project architect
Lydia Marshall, radiates from the front entry, which acts
as a pause between the private and public wings in this
compact design. Set in a clearing among the trees, the
owner desired a simple, peaceful environment in which
to live surrounded by her collection of antique textiles.
The retreat is meant to join her urban sensibilities, her
reverence for art, and the presentation and place of art in
the natural world.

The movement of light throughout the house is of
primary importance in displaying textiles, as well as in
the preservation of the delicate fabrics. The interior
design called for the development of tall walls reaching
lofty ceilings, then sloping to very low southern height.
The intersecting planes gave small rewards of niches and
framed walls where the textiles can be hung and high-
lighted, as well as protected from ultraviolet damage. The
functionality of the ever-present Northwest "overhang,"
a long and broad eave designed to keep the rain away
from the exterior siding and the sun rays away from sen-
sitive interior spaces, is again appreciated here.

Apart from the gallery-like criteria, the owner
asked the architect to experiment with inexpensive,
resource-efficient materials and creative detailing, keep-
ing in mind her allotted budget. High on the owner's
wish list was a desire for asymmetrical design, peaceful
areas, "surprises," and "clean, simple space." She also
requested a bath with exposure to the outdoors and, as a

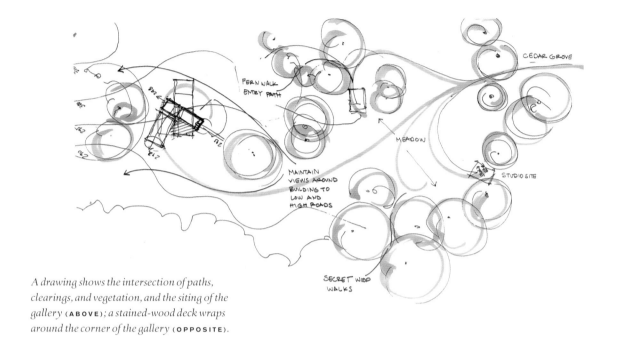

Within the drawing, the following labels appear:

CEDAR GROVE

FERN WALK
ENTRY PATH

MEADOW

STUDIO SITE

MAINTAIN
VIEWS AROUND
BUILDING TO
LOW AND
HIGH ROADS

SECRET WOOD
WALKS

*A drawing shows the intersection of paths,
clearings, and vegetation, and the siting of the
gallery (**ABOVE**); a stained-wood deck wraps
around the corner of the gallery (**OPPOSITE**).*

serene finishing touch, a view of the moon through a skylight above her bed.

The 1,400-square-foot house has two bedrooms, one bath, and an open living area. Framed views create a dialogue with wall-hung textile pieces, while glass corners bring the greenery of the outdoors into interior spaces at the entry, the office, and the bath. The great room is a multipurpose space for cooking, entertaining, and relaxing, as well as enjoying the textiles and artwork. One wall is composed of an attractive system of sliding panels for storage—which alternately conceal and reveal a playful composition of high windows—and cabinetry with stained plywood and metal surfaces. The office converts

to guest quarters and has windows on three sides that open onto slender alder trees against a backdrop of darker, sturdier cedars. A small sunny deck wraps around one corner of the house, gradually descending to ground level. The focus of the master bedroom comes from the natural light admitted from the large skylight, while the master bath features a separate bathing area with a tub surrounded by glass tiles and views into the trees.

This five-acre site of rolling wooded hills on Whidbey Island is a home to wildlife, a place where deer stop and listen to their companions in the forest. This special house allows the forces of art and nature to meet, mingle, and reveal its owner's resourcefulness in the woods.

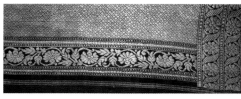

The owner's collection of textiles is a pleasant counterpoint to the angular contours of the retreat (OPPOSITE); the north wall of the great room (TOP LEFT); antique textiles from the owner's collection (BOTTOM LEFT); a pocket door separates the study (or guest room) from activities in the great room (RIGHT).

HOOD CANAL CABIN

OWNERS: Ethan Meginnes and Alexandra Loeb

ARCHITECT: Castanes Architects

PHOTOGRAPHER: MICHAEL MOORE

This cabin sits on a forty-five acre site (**OPPOSITE**); *the loft bedroom and "study" offer a bit of privacy in the tiny cabin* (**ABOVE**).

PERCHED HIGH ABOVE THE GROUND in its lonely habitat, where it resembles a large-scale sculpture in the landscape, this cabin is reached by a gangplank that can be raised and lowered. The many window angles of this tiny 800-square-foot house allow light to enter the living space through as many as sixteen different directions. This Mondrian-inspired design of the windows creates a sunlit corner in the main room and offers various snap-shots of the outdoors, from the busy waters of the canal to the heavily crusted bark of nearby cedar trees. The cabin was designed for a couple who are avid lovers of the out-doors and participate whenever possible in vigorous sports like mountain biking and track cycling. As the

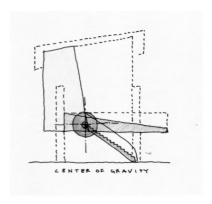

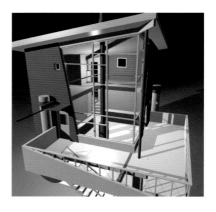

A sketch of the "gear" that raises and lowers the ladder (TOP); a model of the design, showing concrete pilings, ladder, and wraparound deck (BOTTOM); the interior first-floor living room is bright and airy (OPPOSITE).

architect points out, "Their escapist yearnings are reflected in the unusual material choices they've made."

A clearly visible example is the clear-sealed exterior cedar siding alongside eggplant-colored fiber-cement panels. Inside, the rich color is an ideal choice to offset the clear-sealed birch surfaces. A galvanized-steel stair wraps around a central column, leading to two sleeping lofts, and behind the column a secret sleeping nook awaits special visitors. A two-story bookcase and the kitchen casework reflect the lines of the maple railings. This house is a carefully placed gem on a forty-five-acre site that runs along a quarter mile of waterfront. Tucked deep into a ravine, the cabin faces west with a view to the Olympic Mountains. Held aloft by four massive concrete columns, the positioning works to solve several design concerns. The columns are designed to function as do steel and wood pilings when under forces that accompany the impact of swells and churning waves. Although the cabin isn't constructed over water, it is in the midst of large, imperceptibly moving land masses similar to ocean swells. Eventually, the land will push against the concrete pilings, which are braced for this inevitable meeting of nature and architecture. The structure is designed to respect both the geologic timeline of the earth's movement by the use of the more permanent materials in its base, and also, the more fleeting timeline of individual human occupancy, as represented by the small, fragile use of wood above the pilings.

The open space below the structure creates a convenient place to park a car, and the elevated design provides a simple and elegant solution for the security and protection of the building. At the close of each holiday here and in preparation for departure to the city, the motorized exit stairway is lifted, drawbridge fashion, sealing the unit until the next visit.

The kitchen counter converts to a table for four (LEFT); angular windows frame trees and water views (OPPOSITE).

*A small wood stove warms the cabin (**OPPOSITE**); morning espresso and a journal at the writing desk (**RIGHT**).*

PT. HADLOCK
SAILING CABIN

ARCHITECT: Eggleston l Farkas, Architects

PHOTOGRAPHER: JOHN DiMAIO,

        EGGLESTON l FARKAS, ARCHITECTS

*The sailing cabin on the shores of Pt. Hadlock with Skunk Island in the distance (**OPPOSITE**); the sailing marina is part of the lure of the cabin (**ABOVE**).*

THERE IS LITTLE THAT ARCHITECTS ENJOY MORE than clients who keep returning, and the owners of this sailing cabin are an architect's dream come true. They depend on Eggleston Farkas Architects to provide order to their recreational activities, their pleasures, and, to some degree, their standard of living. Eggleston Farkas has designed not only this beachfront sailing and water sports cabin for them, but also their cross-country skiing and mountain biking cabin in Washington's Methow Valley (see page 186), as well as their primary residence in a northeast Seattle neighborhood. The two recreational cabins, as well as their impeccable city home, demonstrate this couple's preference for honest and efficient design.

*A view of the marina provides entertainment when not sailing (**OPPOSITE**); the plan and elevation of cabin (**RIGHT AND BELOW**).*

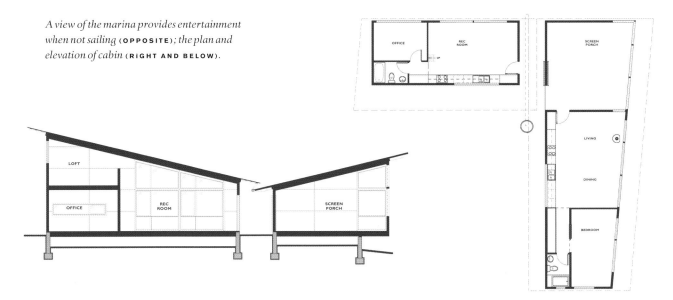

The clients' waterfront property is located on a curve in the beach of Pt. Hadlock on the irregular shoreline of Puget Sound, in a community governed by ferry schedules and tide tables. The cabin overlooks a marshy wetland and a small marina to the northeast. It has a freshwater stream seeking its way down through the property to the harbor. To the west, the jagged peaks of the Olympic Mountains can be seen over the tidewater cove. For even more visual interest, there is Skunk Island, a mere five hundred feet offshore, and an old mill and Port Townsend in the distance. Watching the ferries breeze through a purple-orange sunrise is a genuine balm for the soul. Sailing, windsurfing, and kayaking are all available.

Sited to take advantage of all that can be seen and heard, the cabin's two major design elements form an L. The main living space is oriented to face the marina and the wildlife habitat of the wetlands. In the enclosure of the building, where it makes a ninety-degree turn, the overlapping legs of the design make a lovely spot for the large screened-in porch. The views from the porch—a favorite spot for casual meals and relaxing—include the regular flurry of flashing sails and the underwings of gulls reflecting the afternoon sunlight.

The concrete base creates a level area on the sloping site, providing storage for the small sailboat in the cabin. The wood-frame structure is clad in cement board panels throughout, unifying the interior with the exterior. The interior is warmed and energized by the use of light maple on the angled ceiling and interior cabinetry. Slate floors complete the natural palette and add a rustic finish to this well-defined and stylish marine retreat. The owners' devotion to modern design and to preserving the natural environment always presents their architects with an unambiguous strategy when designing for them.

A galley kitchen shares space with the living and dining area (**OPPOSITE**); *the large screened-in porch is perfect for gathering after an afternoon of water recreation* (**ABOVE**).

KITSAP PENINSULA
GUEST CABIN

ARCHITECT: Rohleder Borges Fleming Architecture
PHOTOGRAPHER: JOHN DiMAIO

The guest cottage amidst the growing garden (**OPPOSITE**);
*a small pool and fountain will be the focus of the garden
landscape* (**ABOVE**).

THIS PICTURESQUE GUEST COTTAGE was built on the grounds of an existing weekend house. The cottage is a short distance from the main house, which has extensive views of Puget Sound and the Olympic Mountain range to the west. Lush native vegetation grows in clusters and pockets around the main lawn. The cottage, however, is an integral part of more immediate surroundings. A large greenhouse and gardens are planned adjacent to the guest house. A stone path and several small, private stone patios connect the cottage court to the greenhouse and nursery beds. The two-story structure sits in tranquility among ornamental grasses, blossoming herbs, Japanese lace-leaf maples, magenta and white perennials, a meadow, and a forest.

The architects employed a familiar geometry—the tic-tac-toe layout—that efficiently cultivates ease of movement within the cottage from room to room. It also contributes to the easy access between the outside decks and the living room, kitchen, and bedroom or from the loft, which has its own stairway entrance. The first-floor interior living space opens onto a broad wraparound porch, which includes a screened sleeping area under a wide, tropical-looking overhang. For guests, day or night, rain or shine, this is choice camping. The second floor features lanternlike light wells that connect the four corners of the loft with the main space below. They also double as "night buoys" to help guide visitors to their upstairs accommodations.

Materials and structure are simple and natural. Columns and beams are composites of fir and steel. Floors, decks, and ceilings are made from one-and-a-half-inch fir planks. Exterior walls are clad with fiber-cement panels. The roofs are made of galvanized metal, a material that reflects the color of the sky and matches the vernacular regional farm buildings.

*The upper level sleeping area (**LEFT**); a detail of the second-floor ceiling (**RIGHT**); the cottage living room and decks are designed to arouse interest in the surrounding natural vegetation and exotic greenhouse varieties (**OPPOSITE**).*

*The door leading to the outdoor pool and fountain (**RIGHT**); the open air bath (**BOTTOM LEFT**); the gleaming tiles and wood floors of the bath (**BOTTOM RIGHT**); a view of Puget Sound from the grounds (**OPPOSITE**).*

DECATUR ISLAND HAVEN

OWNERS: Christian Grevstad and Terris Draheim
ARCHITECT: George Suyama Architects
PHOTOGRAPHER: CLAUDIO SANTINI

The cabin nestles up to rocks for a spectacular view of the San Juan Islands (OPPOSITE); the approach to this dream house with the shed on the left and the cabin on the right (ABOVE).

IN THE MID-1990S, while flying over the San Juan Islands, designer Christian Grevstad's instincts led him to alert his pilot that they were off course and lost. As the pilot corrected the flight path, Grevstad glanced down at a flowering meadow sitting atop a high bluff. Below him lay the site he had envisioned for his ideal island getaway. He headed for Seattle, where he did the necessary foot-work, and found that the price was right. He later realized that years earlier he had hiked up the face of the very mountain that led to this meadow, but he had not ventured over the top where the meadow flourished. Having spent much of his life in the San Juans, Grevstad can navigate both the air and waterways of the islands with ease.

The large sliding walls, broad overhang, and narrow clerestory windows make an attractive shed structure.

This is where he goes to simplify his life, when he can free himself for a few days from the demands of an international design practice.

Grevstad's first step in creating his cabin was to choose an architect of vision, one who shared his belief in simplicity. His design requests were few: the house should mirror the surrounding landscape; it should exude a feeling of relaxation; it should allow for an appreciation of Asian art; and there should be a seamless blend of interior and exterior when the doors open to the vistas under the floating roof.

Nestled atop a tree-covered ridge on Decatur Island, the 1,500-square-foot cabin is composed of three distinct boxlike volumes connected by a simple shed roof. One box structure contains the living room, kitchen, and family rooms; each of the other two boxes is reserved for sleeping quarters. Large windows framed with wood create heated living space between the three volumes and

The largest of the three boxes that comprise the cabin under a shed roof, this rectangle houses the dining room and out-door dining area.

camouflage the building amid the rocks and trees on the other side of the glass.

The liberties of island leisure complement the unadorned natural and stylized materials Grevstad chose. His selection of finishes is compatible with the natural palette: the concrete slab floor is stained a charcoal black; wood-beam ceilings and walls are stained with the tones of the bark of the trees outside. The tints on exterior sid-

ing continue through the inside of the cabin as the walls wrap around the three interior "boxes," whose walls are intended as a background for artwork. The voids and niches inside are for the display of sculptures. Together, the architect and Grevstad also designed a spiral staircase ascending to an open-roof terrace, referred to as the "martini tower," where guests often enjoy a tasty drink called a Lemon Drop (see recipe, page 111).

The design of the cabin and its furnishings does not overwhelm the beauty of the natural environment on the other side of the glass (**OPPO-SITE**); the Asian tansu and basket collection (**RIGHT**); a freehand sketch of the cabin by the architect (**BELOW**).

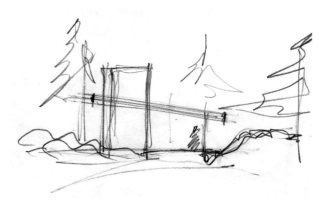

*LEMON DROP

3 sugar cubes
Juice of 1 lemon
1 ¼ oz. citron vodka
¼ oz. Grand Marnier

Place the sugar cubes in a pint glass. Pour in enough lemon juice to cover the cubes; stir until sugar dissolves. Fill the glass with crushed ice. Add the citron vodka and Grand Marnier, and shake six to eight times. Strain into a chilled, sugar-rimmed glass.

*The interior of the dining and sitting unit (**ABOVE**); behind the fireplace is a small interior box housing a bedroom and a hallway leading to the patio (**OPPOSITE**).*

LOCKWOOD
SAN JUAN RETREAT

OWNERS: Jim and Christina Lockwood
ARCHITECT: George Suyama Architects
PHOTOGRAPHER: CLAUDIO SANTINI

The view from the bluff on Lopez Island (OPPOSITE); the reflecting pool between the main and guest houses (ABOVE).

THIS LOVELY LOPEZ ISLAND vacation retreat rests on an inconspicuous bluff on a rambling, twenty-five acre site with spectacular views in all directions, particularly of countless islands in the distance across the water. For years the bluff was a favorite getaway for Jim and Christina Lockwood. They and their friends spent much time there, camping in tents and exploring. Over the years they had learned the path of the sun, the cycles of the seasons, the comings and goings of animals, the changing plant life, the directions of the wind. By the time they chose their architect they already knew exactly where they wanted to build.

Jim and Christina Lockwood look forward to peaceful days at the Lopez Island house, when they can leave

behind the frenetic pace of life in Seattle. The house is divided into two sections, although it looks as if the architect began with the long, exhilarating recreation and relaxation rectangle, and then situated the main house at one end and a private building for friends at the other end. There are ingenious provisions for privacy and for the areas devoted to shared activities and entertainment. For example, the central gathering area is flanked at one end by the kitchen and dining area. Tucked behind the kitchen is a small niche with a daybed and window, which opens onto the patio and pool. And beyond the niche lies the secluded master suite.

Glass on either wall of the open gathering area allows guests to enjoy views and sunsets all the way from the guest house, through the main house, and out to the islands beyond. A design professional, Christina Lockwood selected the furnishings for the 2,600-square-foot retreat, including a coffee table from Gulassa and Company and a dining table from David Smith and Company. It was important to the owners to furnish the space with all the essentials, but the lesson they learned from years of camping was to leave everything else behind. When the sunlight is glittering off the surface of the pool and bouncing onto the walls and ceilings, swaying and sparkling throughout the rooms, one must leave space for a less strenuous experience of nature, too.

*The kitchen and freestanding island disappear into the design (**ABOVE**); views of the islands can be seen through the living room (**OPPOSITE**).*

*The living room receives sunlight through the clerestory windows and the broad roof overhang (**TOP LEFT**); an airy day bed for a quiet hour or two (**TOP RIGHT**); the living area with exposed ceiling beams (**BOTTOM**); the steps past the pool to the guest house (**OPPOSITE**).*

ALKI POINT HOUSE

OWNERS: Steve and Pam Zeasman
ARCHITECT: Arellano/Christofides
PHOTOGRAPHER: MICHAEL MOORE

The urban retreat on Seattle's Alki Point (**OPPOSITE**)*; the top floor living room and deck look out at the Puget Sound waters* (**ABOVE**).

THE ZEASMAN RETREAT is located on the last site that would be built on the west end of Alki Beach, next to a public park. This is where small, old ferries, affectionately named "the mosquito fleet," docked when loading and unloading commuters crossing Puget Sound. Wave-worn pilings, remnants from the early pier, can still be seen at low tide and are a familiar sight throughout the Northwest on rivers, bays, and the Sound.

The Zeasmans, Seattlites who grew up near the Sound, are contractors who had the opportunity to build this house through a revision to a ten-year-old building permit that had carried stipulations affecting any new design.

The three-bedroom, three-and-a-half bath home rises out of the sand, supported on fifty-five steel pin piles protected by riprap on the water side. The lowest level of concrete serves as extra insurance against surging tides. The living spaces orient themselves toward the water with the mountains in the background, with less frequented spaces and circulation on the street side of the house. A compact entry court and stoop provide semi-private space and buffering at the street level.

Their plan evolved into three levels. To take advantage of the views, it has a "living pavilion" located on the top floor, a gabled roof line, deck areas, and open interiors in the main living space. The middle level houses private spaces for sleeping and bathing, while the entry level contains the guest quarters as well as a hot tub just steps away from the parking area in the garage. Each floor was split in a way that responds to the site's slope, allowing for entry to the garage and living space, and access to the beach. The efficient design thus eases the vertical ascent through the home.

Four glazed gable ends support a timber roof above the pavilion space, which is rendered in a contrast of retro Northwest "lodge" materials such as grayed-out wood and flagstone, with contrasting polished stainless-steel railings, fireplaces, and light fixtures. One of the strongest features is the raised corner of the dining room, which appears to float and which opens out onto a deck to provide a seamless indoor-outdoor space.

The retreat is sited on a narrow lot between the street and the shore (**OPPOSITE**)*; the corner walls open to create a canopy over the dining area* (**ABOVE**)*.*

*The living room and dining area are differentiated by elevation and materials (***OPPOSITE***); a sizable kitchen area behind the counter provides an additional gathering place on the upper level (***ABOVE***).*

On the exterior, the pavilion is expressed as a metal clad form perched atop the more rustic wood base of the floors below. Brazilian cherry lines the stair tower and elevator shaft. Windows of both mahogany and aluminum complete the simple yet rich color palette. There are many ingenious touches throughout the home such as the hot tub in the garage, beachside storage, and a range of built-ins that make the compactness of the project efficient and fun.

The owner/contractor and architect collaborated on the design process, with the contractor contributing an enormous amount of time and creativity to the detailing and selection of materials. The problems to be solved throughout the project led to increasingly simple and systematic solutions, so that the end result is remarkably close to the first cocktail napkin sketches.

BAINBRIDGE BOATHOUSE

OWNERS: Kevin and Kristin Eagan
ARCHITECT: William J. Chester
PHOTOGRAPHER: MICHAEL MOORE

*The boathouse on the shore of Bainbridge Island (**OPPOSITE**); details of fused glass in bronze columns are reminiscent of Charles Rennie Mackintosh designs (**ABOVE**).*

TRADITIONALLY, MANY WATERFRONT PROPERTIES on Bainbridge Island had boathouses. Built above the high-tide line, they were used to store small runabouts, rowboats, and paddleboats. Although many of these old buildings have been lost to age and neglect, a few remain, and Kevin and Kristin Eagan's low-bank waterfront property on the west side of the island had one of them.

The Eagans hoped to reconstruct the boathouse as part of an overall renovation. The project began on the site of the existing boathouse structure with the simple idea of providing winter storage for their fourteen-foot runabout. In the summer months, when the little boat could be moored to a buoy in the water, the structure could be

used for other purposes, such as a beach cabana or a quiet place to read or work. The Eagans challenged their architect to design a reconstruction that would have a timeless quality and that would last roughly two hundred years, with normal maintenance, to display quality. Under city regulations, however, this task could be undertaken only within the existing footprint of the original boathouse.

Bill Chester's solution is embodied in a sturdy, craftsman-style gem that blends diverse architectural influences. Chester selected materials designed to resist both the harsh storms coming from the south and the salt spray of the sea. The structural skeleton of the boathouse, for example, is revealed in redwood timbers and bronze columns. The walls and ceiling are tongue-and-groove teakwood. The roof is a Bermuda hip clad in layered copper. The structure rests on a granite sill and a stone base of green Vermont ledge stone.

The interior was finished by local artisans, who relished their participation in this project. There is a bronze sink (with running water) mounted in a redwood-and-teak cabinet, sporting a heavy black granite surface and hung with strong bronze brackets. On the opposite wall is an adjustable-height counter, which can be used either as a serving bar or as a bench. When the boat is being stored, it can be easily folded away. Two matching cabinets—one conceals the circuit breakers, the other stows glassware and wine—flank the entry. The boathouse is

Arts and crafts, Asian, and modern influences combine to form the timeless boathouse.

A lovely place to enjoy an evening on the beach (**ABOVE**); *tongue-and-groove teak walls and ceiling sit atop Vermont ledge stone and marble flooring* (**OPPOSITE**).

smart-wired and contains a foldaway desk for Kevin, a technology professional, who enjoys spending some of his working hours in this beautiful setting.

What most makes the boathouse shimmer and glow is the glasswork by Mesolini Glass Studio. Fused glass squares, in a pattern evoking the designs of Charles Rennie Mackintosh, are set into the bronze columns, and the double front doors have leaded glass panels across their tops. Corners of mitered glass and a clerestory circumnavigating the structure give the roof the illusion of floating above the structure, supported only by the four bronze columns. At night, the interior lighting flows out through the glass patterns, corners, and clerestory, causing the entire boathouse to resemble a twinkling jewel box.

GUEMES ISLAND CABIN

OWNERS: Bruce and Laura Saunders

ARCHITECT: Miller Hull Partnership;
Robert Hull, design principal

PHOTOGRAPHER: JOHN DiMAIO

The Guemes Island hideaway (**OPPOSITE**); *the deck under the trees overlooking Puget Sound* (**ABOVE**).

MILLER HULL'S MOST RECENT vacation house, on Guemes Island, north of Seattle, is situated in the woods with nothing man-made in sight, yet it is only a quick eighty-minute drive from the city. The owners found and fell in love with the site, which slopes steeply down to a rocky beach. A three-quarter-mile stretch of Puget Sound separates the beach from the next island. The property is forested with evergreens and native plants; bald eagles circle overhead and nest nearby. Basalt boulders emerge from the ground under blankets of moss. A simple footpath welcomes visitors to this quintessential Northwest cabin.

Designed by Bob Hull, the plan consists of a long bar structure for the main house. The roof structure is

The kitchen shed on the side of the cabin leads to a deck (**OPPOSITE**); *the front entry and porch lead through a hanging door to the work space* (**ABOVE**).

exposed, and the two-by-eight-foot framing is rigorously laid out. The cabin is so specifically designed for its site that decks curve around the rock and the walls roll up to create the pleasure of an insect-free wilderness.

The program was simple and was based on a desire for natural light to be available and set in contrast to the darkness of the forest. This was accomplished with a bold and fluent adaptation of extruded, double-glazed material at the roof ridge, which converts the peak of the room's ceiling into a continuous skylight admitting natural light throughout the length of the long interior room from early morning until late afternoon. Views to the coast and the mountains are enhanced by the placement of wood-framed, floor-to-ceiling windows.

Flexible rooms and outdoor porches are part of the cabin's charm. For instance, in response to the owner's desire to be able to "use" the site, the east wall, which is a glazed garage door, can be rolled up, transforming the

*The living and dining area with overhead light coming through the skylight (**LEFT**); large windows frame forest views and admit available sunlight (**RIGHT**); views of the waters of the Sound (**OPPOSITE**).*

workroom into an open den with a fresh, intimate relationship with the trees and meadow outside. A Murphy bed converts the space to a guest room. A small railing and a very broad overhang protect the opening, and on warm rainy days one can be inside—with a fire, if desired—and still enjoy the rain. A rust-colored "lean-to" on the west side of the cabin contains cooking and serving areas, and an entry porch. A window and dormer have views up the hill to the entry path, while a porch and its

steps connect with a trail leading down the hill to the beach. The exterior consists of metal walls and roofs, cedar battens, and hemlock trim.

This summer vacation house was planned with the future in mind and awaits the visits of extended family members and friends. Its simple innovations and materials satisfy the essentials of life and much more, that it will be a favorite place in their world for years to come.

*The interior work space and garage door (**LEFT**); the work space in the meadow (**OPPOSITE**).*

TEMPIETTO

OWNERS: Thomas and Elaine Bosworth

ARCHITECT: Thomas L. Bosworth, FAIA

PHOTOGRAPHER: MICHAEL SKOTT

The cottage is reminiscent of a classical Greek temple on a hill (**OPPOSITE**); *oversized 7-¹/₂-foot windows emphasize the interior appointments* (**ABOVE**).

THERE IS A NATURAL CURIOSITY about the kind of secret getaways architects design for themselves. A solid architectural career—as well as a dedication to archaeology, art history, and travel—reveal themselves in Thomas Bosworth's simple and bold forms. When Bosworth found a hill that seemed to be calling for his retreat to be built upon it, he envisioned the classic spaciousness of ancient Mediterranean temples. This might be the king's hall, where the gods were welcomed with the finest hospitality. Elaine Bosworth, an antiques dealer, furnishes their homes with objects from the couple's worldwide travels. They believe that buildings and forms, as well as furnishings, can flourish through a state of historical flux, changing with time.

The project consists of a traditionally framed 260-square-foot gatehouse and a 1,050-square-foot vacation cottage on San Juan Island. The narrow gatehouse forms one segment of a thick "hedge" that separates the parking area from the landscape around the cottage while providing a pedestrian connection between itself and the cottage. Clad in tight-knot vertical cedar boards, the gatehouse rises with the terrain, creating the perception of a forced perspective along its surface and opposite the parking area. A nine-foot-wide barn door slides open to reveal a central entry slot through the building, a small guest room to the left, and a bath and tool storage to the right, all framed simply with exposed two-by-four studs, skip sheathing, fir plank floors, and cedar shingles. As it descends through this slot and toward the cottage, the site has been preserved in its natural condition.

The twenty-four-by-forty-four-foot axial cottage was conceived as a type of Greek *megaron,* which is simply a large room in plan, and was placed along a path

between tall fir trees on the north and the rocky, moss-covered slope rising from fields to the south. Broad steps lead to the porch and into a great room containing the kitchen, dining, and seating areas. Framed by book-shelves, paired window seats provide cozy spots for viewing the fields and Puget Sound beyond. Although modest in size, the cottage is filled with natural light from tall, true divided-light windows and from a generous light monitor placed in the hall connecting the great room to the private bedroom and bath areas. The cottage is constructed with two-by-six-foot wood framing, poured-in-place concrete columns, standard wood roof trusses, and clad with one-by-eight-inch rough cedar channel siding and a cedar shingle roof.

There is a sense that from the portico, an offering is being made to the gods. Perhaps they will come down for an afternoon of frolicking.

Tempietto *is firmly placed on a stone ridge.*

*The cabin is appointed with items collected by the owners (**OPPOSITE**); a love of shaker design influences the cabin's interior (**ABOVE**).*

The sun bounces off open shelving across large windows (**OPPOSITE**); the bedroom has a provincial touch (**LEFT**); simplicity in the bath (**BELOW**).

The gatehouse separates
the parking area from the
landscape surrounding
the cottage (OPPOSITE);
a well-equipped tool shed
is part of the gatehouse,
along with a guest room
and bath (RIGHT).

the east side (of the mountains)

THE CASCADE RANGE was formed back in the days when mountains were people and Klickitat (Mount Adams) and Wyeast (Mount Hood) were fighting over the beautiful maiden Loowit (Mount St. Helens). Wyeast and Klickitat met at the now-fallen Bridge of the Gods over the Columbia River and hurled stones and fire at each other. Other mountains, such as the Three Sisters in Central Oregon, were marching up from the south to join the battle, but when Coyote destroyed the bridge and ended the fray, they stopped where they were and did not move again. Together with Mount Jefferson, Mount Washington, Mount Rainier across the river, and other massive peaks, they shield the inland plateaus and high desert from the rain-bearing westerlies. Clouds sweeping in from the Pacific are borne upward by the mountains, and their moisture falls in the green valleys, leaving the eastern slopes dry.

CABIN AT ELBOW COULEE

OWNER: Tom Lenchek

ARCHITECT: Balance Associates, Architects;
Tom Lenchek, principal designer

PHOTOGRAPHER: STEVE KEATING PHOTOGRAPHY

*The cabin at Elbow Coulee is perfect for ski weekends (**OPPOSITE**); in warm weather, the outdoor shower is an invigorating start to the day (**ABOVE**).*

IN SUMMER AND IN WINTER, this cabin in north central Washington is an all-around winner for welcome, comfort, sport, and adventure. The owner and architect, Tom Lenchek, gave special attention to details that more than make up for being away from the conveniences of city life. For example, he has incorporated both a sauna and an outdoor bath into the design of this 1,400-square-foot structure. Located in the mountains, the cabin sits on a south-facing slope with views to the south and east. In summer there are glorious wildflowers covering the meadow and sunsets over the mountains. Winter provides a landscape of powdery snow, ideal for skiing and sledding.

Lenchek used rough materials—logs, sawn beams, rough-formed concrete, and corrugated metal—to reflect the cabin's raw and untamed surroundings. The cabin is built on two levels. A lower terrace contains the living, dining, and kitchen areas in one open volume. The upper level becomes the back of the living area and the floor of the bedroom and bath level. Each bedroom has its own small terrace planted with wildflowers and herbs. Two eight-by-eight-foot wood-framed sliding glass walls open the living space onto the terrace and the outdoors. The main terrace is planted with native wildflowers and has a small water garden with meditative boulders.

Lenchek designed the cabin with sustainability in mind, and his choice of materials reflects this. The house is sided with one-by-twelve-inch boards, weathered more than sixty years, that were salvaged from a water irrigation ditch. Lenchek is confident that when cleaned and treated with a sealer, they will last another sixty years. The roof purlins are made from lodge pole pine logs, which come from forest thinning. Much of the remaining materials are engineered products used on the ceiling, wall finishes, and stair treads. Most of the high-performance glazing faces south and east to allow for passive solar heating. The east-facing glazing provides morning warming, which brings comfort even in the summer when nighttime lows often drop into the thirties. Here in the mountains, what is considered essential are not the things you left behind, but what is gained from simplicity.

A sliding wall converts living space to an outdoor experience with endless vistas.

*Floor-to-ceiling glass walls surround the living and dining area. The wall to the right of the wood stove opens to the outdoors (**ABOVE**); the owner's choice of materials supports his belief in the necessity of sustainable architecture (**OPPOSITE**).*

*Each bedroom opens onto a terrace (**LEFT**); this terrace has an herb garden in the spring and summer (**OPPOSITE**).*

CHESNUT RETREAT

OWNERS: Anna and Charles Chesnut

ARCHITECT: Thomas L. Bosworth, FAIA

PHOTOGRAPHER: ART GRICE

*A ranch retreat in the pastures of eastern Washington (**OPPOSITE**); the house's spread seems as broad as the plains (**ABOVE**).*

AT 2,400 SQUARE FEET, this country ranch house satisfies its owners' desire for more sunshine and the slower pace of eastern Washington. Seated in the midst of fifty acres of pasture and grassland of Kitittas County, the house and tower have a commanding view of the surrounding territories. With an eye toward symmetry, the public spaces of the house lie in the center, where they are flanked by the more private spaces on either side. The south face of the house is an enfilade, an interconnected series of rooms that align to create a vista through the spaces when all the doors between them are opened. This is an ingenious adaptation of a seventeenth-century arrangement that was a feature in French baroque

Wood is used extensively on the main floor and upper level (**LEFT**); *a section of the main house and reading tower* (**OPPOSITE TOP**); *the site plan* (**OPPOSITE BOTTOM**).

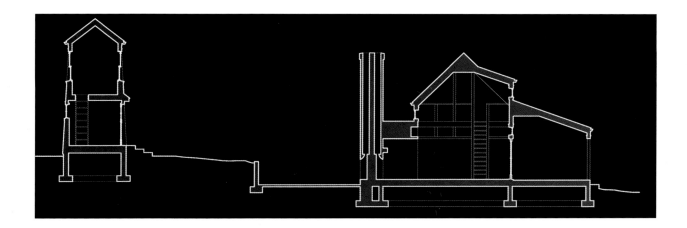

palaces. The space is lined with double-hung fir windows that gather southern light from the porches and the pasture. An eighteen-foot accordion door divides the central great room and screen porch, but can be rolled back to allow the great outdoors to spill into the house. In the winter, when the screens are replaced with glazed windows, the porch can be used as a solarium.

The owners spend a great deal of time on the porches and terraces lazing in hammocks, watching migrating birds, or enjoying the evenings with friends. A stone-paved terrace behind the house is sunk into a low hillside to preserve views to the north. On axis with the front door is a long hallway that leads outside and beyond to the observation and sleeping tower. The tower features a below-ground wine cellar and sleeping benches surrounded by windows above. Built simply and honestly, its materials include galvanized roofing, cedar siding, fir windows, and clear-sealed cedar paneling throughout the interior. Although ninety minutes east of Seattle, it feels like an escape to a hundred years ago.

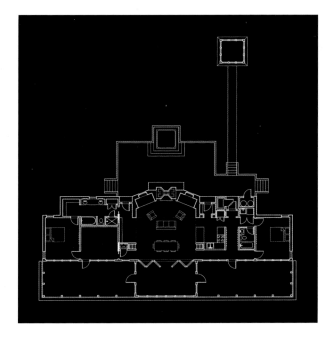

*The living room features window seats, bookshelves, and a perfect fireplace (**ABOVE**); the wide screened-in porches on either side of the central living room provide plenty of outdoor space (**OPPOSITE**).*

BLUE LAKE RETREAT

OWNERS: Dan and Bonnie Wieden

ARCHITECT: Allied Works Architecture;
Brad Cloepfil, partner-in-charge

PHOTOGRAPHER: JOHN DiMAIO

The extraordinary view of Blue Lake as seen from the dining room (**OPPOSITE**); *the old water wheel on the premises* (**LEFT**); *pine needles cover the steps that lead to the entry terrace along the sandalwood stone wall* (**RIGHT**).

IF THERE IS A FAMILIARITY about this retreat in the mountains, it is helpful to know to what extent our individual and collective consciousness has been influenced by its owner, Dan Wieden of the Wieden + Kennedy advertising agency. His are the ads that got us to "Just Do It!" and to contemplate exactly how to renovate a bath with tile and copper wash basins from Ann Sacks. Combine his vision with the architect's, and an unexplored tweak on traditional lodge materials, and the result is something we have never seen before.

Dan and Bonnie Wieden asked the architect to design an intimate space that would also allow for occasional large gatherings. The Wiedens enjoy a wide range of activ-

ities, from weekends on their own to long holidays with lots of family and friends. Surrounded by forty acres of Cascade Range foothills in central Oregon, the site overlooks Blue Lake, the caldera of an ancient volcano. The climactic changes in the region are severe. There are usually three to five feet of snow and high winds in the winter, and summers are so hot and dry that pinecones snap in the heat. The house was built seventy feet above the water, for southern light and spectacular views across the lake to Mount Washington's nearly 8,000-foot summit.

The entry is tucked into a recess, behind thick stone walls and beneath a heavily timbered, inverted umbrella space. Once inside, a turn to the right leads to a large living room and gathering space. The entire south wall of this room opens to views of Blue Lake framed in the nostalgic warmth of recycled fir timbers. In many ways this is the most important space in the house, with dining and cooking areas very close at hand, and terraces at every turn.

Local stone and recycled fir timbers are the primary structural elements. The heavy timber frame lifts the roof over the walls and creates the large overhang that protects the house and the interior courtyard from snow in winter and direct southern sun in summer. The wall of the courtyard is constructed of operable fir panels, fixed glazing, and huge sliding doors that animate the ambiguity between interior and exterior.

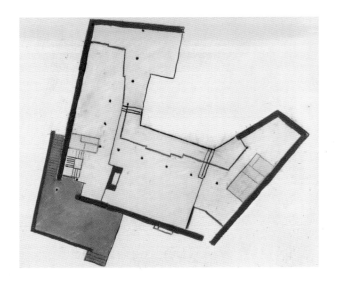

Wood flows from the interior flooring to the exterior decks (**OPPO-SITE**); *the view of the court and outdoor deck* (**TOP**); *the first-level floor plan* (**BOTTOM**).

The bedroom window niche shows the depth of the stone walls and an extensive roof overhang (**LEFT**); *the bedroom has flat sandstone walls and large timber construction* (**BOTTOM LEFT**); *the upper level guest room with fireplace and sleeping nook* (**BOTTOM RIGHT**); *the living room and fireplace with the dining room and deck on the right* (**OPPOSITE**).

The unreserved hush of Central Oregon's Blue Lake

LAKE BILLY
CHINOOK RETREAT

OWNER: Stephen Gomez

ARCHITECT: DiBenedetto/Thompson/Livingstone
Architects; Don Livingstone, principal architect

PHOTOGRAPHER: JOHN DiMAIO

The house is known to its owner as "Desert Green" (**OPPOSITE**); *the colors of the landscape are reflected in the choice of materials* (**ABOVE**).

LAKE BILLY CHINOOK, which is formed by the impounded waters by Round Butte Dam at the confluence of the Metolius, Deschutes, and Crooked rivers in Oregon, creates a tremendous site for hiking, fishing, and waterskiing in the desert. The lake is named in honor of a Wasco Indian chief, born in approximately 1837. Chinook was one of the chiefs of the Dalles band of Wasco Indians and was a signer of the Treaty with the Tribes of Middle Oregon in 1855. In the mid-1860s, he served as a first sergeant in Captain John Darragh's Indian Scouts, during the Shosone Indian War. Surrounded by wilderness and national forests, the lake is in the Three Rivers recreational area, twenty miles west of Madras, in central Oregon's desert country.

Lake Billy Chinook, 850 feet below (**ABOVE**); *junipers and sage fill the view of Mount Jefferson to the west* (**OPPOSITE**).

This retreat was named Desert Green by its owner and architect to denote their efforts to build a sustainable building. The house, guest house, and utility shed sit atop the canyon walls of the lake. The main house and guest quarters are shouldered along the mesa rim and have uninterrupted views of Mount Jefferson and Mount Hood, and the waters of the lake 850 feet below. Among the juniper and sage, shade is at a premium. Thus, a ten-foot-wide porch flows out from a dogtrot breezeway surrounding the house to make ample opportunities for outdoor activities out of the sun's reach.

Corrugated-metal roofing and culvert-clad columns pick up farm building vernacular of the local area. Colors

for the board- and batt- and stucco-clad building were derived from plants, rocks, and lichen on the site. The 2,000-square-foot house contains a variety of sustainable materials and technologies. Since there is no electricity available at the site, a twenty-four-square-foot photovoltaic collector on the south-oriented utility buildings sends its charge to an array of batteries that store power to be converted into 120 volts for lighting and appliances. Consequently, outlets, lights, and appliances were planned with a strict electrical budget for the house. Propane powers the cooking, refrigeration, and radiant-heating systems. Cork, stained concrete, and sea grass–carpeted floors accentuate the cool interior.

The open kitchen area and living room (**LEFT**); *the living room* (**OPPOSITE**).

BROKEN TOP
CASA MONTAÑA

ARCHITECTS: MCM Architects, Robert S. Moreland
INTERIORS: Rose Capestany, RCI Interiors
PHOTOGRAPHER: ROBERT PISANO

Casa Montaña faces the golf course.

THE NORTH-SOUTH LINE of the Cascade Range divides Oregon, separating the high desert on the east from the rainforest and temperate farmland of the western valleys. It is really two parallel ranges. The older one, which dates from eight to forty-five million years ago, is now considered the Cascade foothills. The younger range, formed only five million years ago, is known as the High Cascades and is made up of relatively isolated volcanic peaks. Although some of its volcanoes are believed to be extinct, several, including Mount Hood, Mount Jefferson, and the South Sister, are dormant and may erupt again. Broken Top, as its name suggests, is a jagged series of peaks. Its exploded-looking contour, which was

181

actually formed by glaciers, makes it an easily identifiable landmark for hikers exploring the high country meadows and lava flows west of Bend, Oregon.

Casa Montaña, a mountain getaway for family and friends, is located in a golf course community west of Bend. The house was built around a courtyard to create privacy that would otherwise be compromised by the large houses on either side. A courtyard entry is built around a swimming pool, which has the natural look and feel of a pool of varying depths set in the native rock, and is enhanced by waterfalls. In the midst of the native rock a hot tub re-creates the pleasures of Oregon's early twentieth-century hot springs.

The architect, who calls this retreat style "Cascadian," used a variety of materials—logs, shingles, stucco, and stone—to provide a mountain lodge feeling to the house. The interiors, by Rose Capestany, heighten the charm through her distinctive selection of furnishings. Intimate vignettes within the interior are framed by distressed dark woods with an attractive patina. A separate bunk house off the front courtyard is the perfect place to put up a bundle of teens waiting to go skiing or golfers planning a getaway, with the large kitchen and its pizza oven conveniently near the media room.

The entry to the house is carefully orchestrated. There is no hint from outside the gate as to what lies within. Through the gate, beyond the pool in the courtyard, is a glass-enclosed gallery that runs parallel to the pool, and leads to the great hall and to a sculptural spiral stair culminating in another view. Once inside the great hall, one can survey the courtyard in full. On the opposite side of the room is a panorama of the golf course and the mountains. Stone terraces look out upon the mountains and the fairways, and a built-in barbecue and concrete table and banquet complete the setting for outdoor entertaining.

*The entry offers privacy and a view of the pool (**OPPOSITE**); the entry enclave in the evening.*

The spacious casual country kitchen (**ABOVE**); *the living room, staircase, and loft* (**OPPOSITE**).

METHOW VALLEY SKI CABIN

ARCHITECT: Eggleston Farkas Architects

PHOTOGRAPHER: JIM VAN GUNDY

*This cross-country ski cabin slips into the landscape (**OPPOSITE**); a dining area for six offers an eye-level view of skiers passing on the trail (**ABOVE**).*

THIS ORDERLY RETREAT lies in a sparse meadow adjacent to a network of cross-country trails on the Methow Valley floor in eastern Washington. It is a base for cross-country skiing in winter and mountain biking during warmer seasons. The owners wanted a place that would easily accommodate as many as six to eight skiers or bikers *and* their equipment for a weekend getaway. The key to this kind of togetherness is private sleeping quarters. The cabin has three levels. The lower level is a bunking area. Kitchen, dining, and living areas share the main level with a deck at one end of the space and an entry protected from the weather at the opposite end. Here, floor-to-ceiling windows allow a "see-through" of the entire cabin.

*The entry was designed to accommodate skis and other equipment (**ABOVE**); a view of the landscape through the cabin (**OPPOSITE**).*

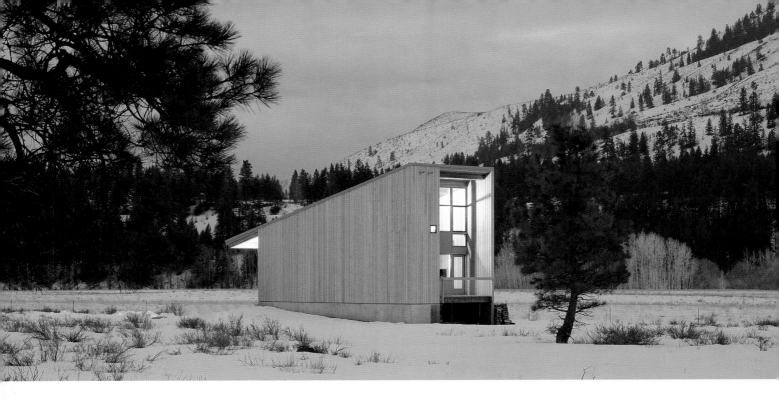

*The cabin at dusk. The roofline mimics the slope of the hills (**ABOVE**); the lower dining area and upper loft (**OPPOSITE**).*

The upper level contains a sleeping loft tucked under the high end of the sloping shed roof. The building is aligned with the valley and has excellent views at either end. A slot window—positioned for seated viewing—frames skiers gliding past.

The shed roof echoes the slope of the surrounding hills and allows accumulating snow to slide off easily. There are no roof penetrations, and the simple form eliminates ridges and valleys that might be susceptible to leaks. The shed creates a protected entry porch at the low end (its steel details were designed for ease of fabrication by local agricultural welders) and a sleeping loft at the high end. The entry stair on the side of the cabin remains snow-free even as snow avalanches dramatically off the end of the roof.

The interior is crisp yet flowing, with nooks for writing, mapping trails, and reading. There is also an efficient, galley-style kitchen tucked under the stair, but still within conversation range and perfectly equipped for the preparation and enjoyment of a robust early breakfast. This cabin has been praised by the AIA Design Award Jury members as "a return to the roots of Northwest architecture; going back to the roots with a simple distilled language, in a beautifully stripped-down version." The architects are recognized as true emerging voices, in fact, as "lone riders on the prairie." This project shows why.

The upper loft bedroom with a built-in map-reading area (**ABOVE**); *the galley kitchen is tucked under the stairs* (**OPPOSITE**).

MAZAMA CABIN
(UNDER CONSTRUCTION)

OWNERS: Dave and Wendy Walter
ARCHITECT: Nils Finne
CONTRACTOR: Rick Mills
PHOTOGRAPHER: NILS FINNE

The house under construction in the snow (**OPPOSITE**); *the stonework reveals the power of the cabin's design* (**ABOVE**).

THE MAZAMA CABIN continues architect Nils Finne's inquiry into the lyrical qualities of wood and stone. The partially built structure now waits quietly, partly buried in snow, for the excitement of spring, when construction will resume. As we imagine this cabin going up, the Montana ledge stone on exterior walls really sings solo. The radiance of workmanship is conspicuous in its solitude. The apt precision of stones, which surround where the windows and doors will be placed, makes clear the strength of this base in supporting what will be built above it. The exterior porches are also stone, while the interior floor is cast concrete with inlaid strips of stone mosaic.

Structural intricacies abound in wood and stone (**OPPOSITE**)*; the roof line begins steeply at the peak and breaks into a gentle slope* (**ABOVE**)*.*

The deep roof overhangs are already doing their job of providing for shelter and welcome. The pitch of the roof and slope of the eaves are dazzling to behold. A series of complex wooden trusses provide the major ordering element of the design. Stone walls of split-face Montana ledge stone support the trusses. The roof line begins very steeply at the peak, then breaks into a gentle slope over a nine-foot-deep stone porch that is continuous on both sides of the cabin. The broad porches will give protection from the heavy winter snow and will create a cool, shady place to meditate during the summer months.

Construction of the cabin began in May 2000, after a long planning and process, which was extended when the construction start window of May to June was missed during the first year. Because of heavy winter snowfall, foundation work in the region usually must begin in early summer. The clients, Dave and Wendy Walter, are personal friends of the architect's, which allowed them to communicate with extra candor and directness, a benefit for all involved and a great aid in such a project. The floor plan shows a straightforward open space containing the living, dining, and kitchen areas at the southwest end, and bedrooms with a loft at the northeast end. A bridge to the loft goes past the kitchen and ends in a stairway close to the front door. The architect relied gratefully on the contractor, Rick Mills, for his expertise with the snow loads and cold temperatures of this valley.

conclusion

IN A REGION where forests historically provided wood and the mountains and glaciers gave stone, construction relied for generations on traditional methods and available materials. The innovative use of salvaged, recycled, and reincorporated materials continues to be important to Northwest architecture.

The final house in this book reflects a commendable effort for co-existence on this planet. No blasting was done; no trees were sacrificed. The traditional building materials are here, and they are put to use with more sustainable products. But equally as remarkable about the house is an interior plan in which daily activities are not inhibited by a design decree. Action spills from the center of the house in every direction, and personal paths conveniently bypass others. The design has a legion of exits and entrances that cartwheel unself-consciously out of the sides of the building. Each space leads to the next, creating the sensation of expansion. This is a pivotal piece of Northwest architecture. The ancient argument between the poets and the philosophers about human life and how to live it can be invigorated by the lessons used in its design, which is less concerned with ritual than with the individual experience.

SUB-POP FUTURE

OWNERS: Hannah Parker and Bruce Pavitt
ARCHITECTS: und l Jerry Garcia l Monte Antrim
PHOTOGRAPHER: MICHAEL MOORE

The house is a welcome reinterpretation of contemporary design (**OPPOSITE**)*; bookshelves in the unusual, brass-clad study* (**ABOVE**).

IT MAY BE PRESUMPTUOUS to think this retreat is a model for the architecture of the twenty-first century—it's early yet. The design of the house, built on Orcas Island, in the San Juans, for Bruce Pavitt, Hannah Parker, and their two children, was meant to investigate its own purpose, an idea that reverberates through the completed structure, without taking itself too seriously. It was and is a complex investigation. The contractor, Jonathan White, who eventually agreed to build it, at first felt that this was a "subversive" design and came close to passing on the project. He was worried. He believed "the risks seemed endless." For starters, the design seemed to go in every direction and angle; the specifications called for no less than seven exterior materials. The materials seemed to collide with one another—there was no obvious "order," to their placement. Reason enough to move on, perhaps; but in a spirit of adventure, he caved and let the apparent mischievousness of it all unleash his inner terror. He began building a house that would teach him to think in new ways about what he was building.

Bruce Pavitt is the cofounder of Seattle's Sub-Pop Records and does not shy away from new forms. He knew from his experience with grunge rock that form is not separable from philosophical content. As a yoga teacher, Hannah, too, knew this. Bruce and Hannah, drawing on their work, and in collaboration with Jerry and Monte, plotted a precise course to reach the composed inner-core of this intellectually challenging task. Their vision would change the way ordinary things appear and the way ordinary things are experienced. The architects used both refined and deliberately "shoddy," finishes. Experimentation was going to be a major part of the project.

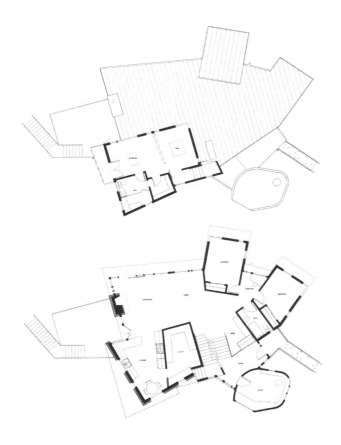

The house, on thirty acres near the top of a hill on Orcas Island, nearly hovers above a granite knoll, rising then sloping toward the waters of Puget Sound, with a view of the mountains in the distance. The design for the house began to take shape around the less obvious landscape; a copse of trees on the meadow's edge, one shapely Madrona, and a bird's-eye view of a rock, which looks like the back of a surfacing whale. The rock formations breaching the crust would not be blasted for foundations. Rather, a topographical template of the mass, density, and elevations of the sloping site was made. The design took into account the variations in elevation, and the stone base of the building simply rose from the slope. Jerry says that prior to construction there was a small concavity in the stone where rain water pooled. It was important to Jerry that this place remain undisturbed, and the projecting spaces that are the children's rooms were designed around it. During construction, a scupper was placed to gather the rain water and allow it to flow back into its own natural rock bowl. This focused conscientiousness is repeated dozens of times throughout the design. The exterior is the result of what happens inside the space. Windows, shapes and colors, roof angles, and floor levels are not in alignment or formal agreement. Decks, balconies, stairs, steps, and a "gangplank" sprout from mysterious openings. It isn't until one comes to know the interiors that the projections and facades reveal their purposes.

An exterior elevation showing "punched-out" openings with bedrooms on the left and living and meditation levels on the right (**OPPOSITE**); *the first- and second-floor plans* (**ABOVE**).

Inside the house the first-floor level is open and flowing, containing kitchen, dining, and living areas. Two private bedrooms and a bath share the main level. Dual staircases lead up to the next two levels. A stone stair leads to Bruce's favorite room, his "brass-drum" study and library, at the mid-level; and a "private" wood staircase next to it leads to the upper level sleeping area and to the meditation room. The interiors are a flux of materials, curves, colors, and elevations. Everywhere, the properties of the materials used were carefully considered. Laminated bamboo, nontoxic finishes, recycled glass, old doors, and engineered panels reveal an emphasis on sustainability and give an air of aliveness. As the sun moves over the house, the color in the small glass windows adjusts internal moods as an ongoing reminder of the rhythms of the natural world.

This house was specifically chosen as the last one to appear in this book. The boldness of its design is markedly neo-Corbusian, yet it also perpetuates subtle Northwest traditions found in Seattle architect Wendell Lovett's later work. The stair-stepping and opposing-angled roof lines are found in the 1978 Gerald Williams Residence in Seattle, designed by TRA, an established Seattle firm. The stone base supporting a wood structure is the very essence of Northwest design. The fearlessness of this design shows that experimentation is a necessary condition for our future. It is a reminder that the truism stating that form is not separable from content can be exemplified in experimentation and boldness.

The house is supported atop a pedestal of stone that appears to float above the natural granite. The owner reports that the house rode out the large Seattle area earthquake "very smoothly" (**OPPOSITE**); *a view from the entry staircase into the living area* (**RIGHT**).

*The living room area with fireplace. An Inuit carving is at the base of the entry staircase (**OPPOSITE**); the kitchen area features colored glass and bamboo floors (**ABOVE**).*

CHARLES MILLER, COURTESY OF *FINE HOMEBUILDING* MAGAZINE

*A bamboo floor and recycled doors lead to the master bedroom (**LEFT**); an ingenious double stairway that leads to Bruce's study on the left and to Hannah's meditation room on the right (**OPPOSITE**).*

NOTES

1. Lisa M. Steinman. "Calling Upon the Night," *All that Comes to Light* (Corvallis, Oregon: Arrowood, 1989), p. 50.

2. Stephen E. Ambrose. *Undaunted Courage: Meriwether Lewis, Thomas Jefferson and the Opening of the American West* (New York: Simon & Schuster, 1996), p. 318.

3. Spiro Kristof, *A History of Architecture, Settings and Rituals* (New York and Oxford: Oxford University Press, 1985), p. 548.

4. Thomas Vaughan, ed. *Space, Style and Structure, Building in Northwest America*, vol. 1 (Portland: Oregon Historical Society Press, 1973), p. 24.

5. Ibid.

6. Ibid.

7. Rachael Griffin and Sarah Munro, eds. *Timberline Lodge* (Portland: Friends of Timberline, 1978), p. 45.

8. Jo Stubblebine, ed. *The Northwest Architecture of Pietro Belluschi* (New York, 1953), p. 5.

PHOTOGRAPHY CREDITS

Ray Atkeson: p. 14 (TOP)

Peter and Sue Belluschi: p. 11 (TOP)

Dick Busher: pp. 18, 19

Canadian Museum of Civilization: p. 5

John DiMaio: pp. viii, x-xi, xii, 3

Fletcher, Farr & Ayotte Architects: p. 12 (TOP RIGHT, LOWER LEFT, LOWER RIGHT)

Edmund Y. Lee: p. 21

Wendell Lovett, FAIA: p. 22

Museum of History and Industry, Seattle, Washington: pp. 9 (BOTTOM), 10 (TOP LEFT, TOP RIGHT, BOTTOM RIGHT)

Oregon Historical Society, Portland, Oregon: pp. 8, 9 (TOP), 10 (BOTTOM LEFT), 11 (BOTTOM), 12 (TOP LEFT), 13, 14 (BOTTOM LEFT, BOTTOM RIGHT), 16

The Purvis Family: p. 17

Gail Martin Rutherford: p. 23